Coming Out as Sacrament

Chris Glaser

Westminster John Knox Press
Louisville, Kentucky

Scripture quotations, unless otherwise noted, are from
the New Revised Standard Version of the Bible,
copyright © 1989 by the Division of Christian Education
of the National Council of the Churches of Christ
in the U.S.A., and are used by permission.

Book design by Sharon Adams
Cover design by Kevin Darst

First edition
Published by Westminster John Knox Press
Louisville, Kentucky

This book is printed on acid-free paper that meets the American National
Standards Institute Z39.48 standard. ♾

PRINTED IN THE UNITED STATES OF AMERICA
98 99 00 01 02 03 04 05 06 07 — 10 9 8 7 6 5 4 3 2 1

Library of Congress Cataloging-in-Publication Data

Glaser, Chris.
Coming out as sacrament / Chris Glaser. — 1st ed.
p.   cm.
Includes bibliographical references.
ISBN 0–664–25748–8 (alk. paper)
1. Homosexuality—Religious aspects—Christianity.   I. Title.
BR115.H6G57   1998
261.8'35766—dc21   98–20654

Coming Out as Sacrament

Other books by Chris Glaser

Coming Out to God: Prayers for Lesbians and Gay Men, Their Families and Friends

Uncommon Calling: A Gay Christian's Struggle to Serve the Church

The Word Is Out: Daily Reflections on the Bible for Lesbians and Gay Men

Come Home! Reclaiming Spirituality and Community as Gay Men and Lesbians

Unleashed: The Wit and Wisdom of Calvin the Dog

Contents

In thanksgiving to God
for my dear friend and mentor,
Henri J. M. Nouwen

Acknowledgments

A book such as this is never a lone effort. I thank my teachers in school and in ministry who have taught me the nature of sacrament, especially Reverend Henri J. M. Nouwen, to whom this book is dedicated. I thank my teachers in the lesbian and gay community who taught me the nature of coming out, including Reverend William Johnson, who was the first to demonstrate to me that one could even come out as a gay Christian minister. I am grateful to the many who have contributed to this book by offering feedback to presentations, workshops, and retreats on the theme of *Coming Out as Sacrament.* After years of developing the ideas contained here, I am also thankful for the added dimensions that my recent study of René Girard and his school of thought have given my treatment of scapegoats and sacrifice.

I thank my editor Stephanie Egnotovich and others at Westminster John Knox Press who believe in my work and this book, and have been supportive of me and helpful in shaping the book's contents. Thanks be to God for the time, energy, and insights of the initial readers of the manuscript: Reverend Beth Basham, Reverend John Bohrer, Dr. George Lynch, and my lover and partner, Mark King. Thanks, too, for the diligence of copyeditor Gary Lee for his editorial suggestions as well as for making the text clearer to the reader.

I am also aware of the debt I owe to those in the design, marketing, and publicity departments of Westminster John Knox Press, to those booksellers who will provide access to readers, and to book reviewers who will call attention to this effort. Without them, this book would still be in the closet!

Finally, thank you, reader, for sharing my interest in this subject. My prayer is that *Coming Out as Sacrament* will further stimulate the discussion on the sacred meaning of the experience of lesbian, gay, bisexual, and transgendered people, as well as of those who love us.

Chris Glaser
Atlanta, Georgia

Coming Out as Sacrament

What is a sacrament?

"A visible sign of an invisible grace."

Augustine of Hippo

"A reality imbued with the hidden presence of God."

Paul VI

"The fullness of joy is to behold God in everything."

Julian of Norwich

"All of life is a sacrament," the Reverend Ross Greek used to say, gleefully rocking back in his high-backed office chair, his gray-blue eyes smiling beneath his wild white eyebrows. His whole face relaxed at the thought, while his index finger waved in the air with the charismatic force of a drum major's baton rallying a marching band. For a moment, he forgot his excruciating back pain as he was caught up in the central revelation that prompted his innovative ministry at the West Hollywood Presbyterian Church: taking the homeless seriously, listening to disenchanted youth, assisting the mentally disabled, intervening with the addicted, marching for civil rights, working with ex-offenders, serving as peacemaker, providing a place for gays and lesbians, reaching out to prostitutes.

"All of life is a sacrament!" What he meant was that all of life is sacred. He did not mean that it merely had a sacred dimension or a sacred potential. He saw all of life as an epiphany of God's glory, a revelation of the holy. Whenever I have grasped this truth, I have relished life, loved others, glorified God, sought justice. Whenever my grasp weakened, I was caught up in despair, divisions, ingratitude, and injustice.

At heart, it was because Ross and I shared this vision that we ministered side by side. Our gospel was a far cry from my early understandings of faith as a fundamentalist, legalist, and literalist. My horizon had been widened by biblical study and exposure to other religions. A deepening sensitivity to both suffering and pleasure engendered a here-and-now, embodied spirituality that replaced my by-and-by, out-of-body experience of faith. The intellectual foundation for the intuitive faith of my heart had been broadened and strengthened by process thought, a philosophical theology that introduced me to panentheism, the belief that the cosmos is *in* God—distinguished from pantheism, the belief that the cosmos *is* God. The cosmos is, according to panentheism, God's body, God's *incarnation,* to broaden a Christian doctrine. A keen sense of justice grew from my belief that earthly life was thus to be taken seriously, or sacramentally. I came to understand that a spirituality that did not take either the body or the earth sacramentally could allow injustice, and liberation theology appropriately claimed the body politic as part of my spiritual landscape.

Of course, long before my acceptance of the fact, it was largely my being gay that permitted—possibly required—these attitudinal changes, stretching my spiritual imagination to envision the sacramentality imbued in the world. I hope that I would have made the same changes because I was compassionate, but I know that the depth of my compassion emerged from my own feelings of being different, left out, ignored, denied, and rejected. The religion on which I was brought up did not deal sufficiently with noncomformity, sensuality, sexuality, scholarship, other religions, reason, or justice. Yet the *spirituality* embedded in that religion, I would find, has proved able to harmonize all of these.

I still had much to learn in my new pastoral position as director of the Lazarus Project, Ross's and my dreamchild, born in 1977 of our mutual passion to reconcile the church and the gay community. Ross seemed so far *out there,* even for me, who had previously served as the avant garde on pastoral teams both in college and seminary. Our first disagreement occurred in a heated discussion over *heterosexual* marriage, which *he* thought was becoming passé, although he was in a conventional, lifelong marriage with Norma, a saint in her own right.

Leading worship together our first World Communion Sunday in October 1977 attested his sacramental disposition. He preached too long, and, noticing the time, proceeded to end the service without Holy Communion! Norma urgently reminded, "Ross, COMMUNION!" To which he replied, "But we don't have time!" As worshipers departed, I broke off a piece of the Communion bread, grimly and judgmentally thinking, "But we could *take* the time." Especially for *World* Communion Sunday. I had personal reasons for wanting us to take the time: I enjoyed the propinquity of my birthday and this annual, intentional worldwide observance of the sacrament.

Just then, someone came into the sanctuary to tell me I had a phone call. As I entered our fellowship hall, the church members shouted out "Surprise!" and began to sing "Happy Birthday." Ross had been afraid that if we did not move things along, worshipers might leave before the surprise birthday party! To him, it was more *vital*—that is, *spiritual* in the sense of life-giving—to have the party than to observe Communion.

The following Sunday we celebrated the missed Communion as Ross explained his "sacrilegious" decision under the sermon title— you might have guessed—"All of Life Is a Sacrament."

Nine years later I would have occasion to recall Ross's sermon in one of my own, entitled "What Is Our Unique Sacrament?" I delivered it on the Sunday we commemorated the ninth anniversary of the Lazarus Project. The project had accomplished much of its purpose. The West Hollywood Presbyterian Church had been resurrected by the influx of gay and lesbian members. Ross had since retired, and our new pastor was going to be away the day of our observance, which fell on the Sunday of the month that we celebrated Communion. I could not lead Communion because I was not ordained—Presbyterian policy forbad ordination of "self-affirming, practicing homosexuals." We could not find an available minister to lead us in the sacrament, so we had to postpone its observance.

In the sermon on that Sunday, I reflected on the irony: I might have been ordained as a minister in my position as director of the Lazarus Project. Since I could not be ordained because of our denomination's prohibition, the ninth anniversary of the project was also the anniversary of my "non-ordination." As a result, we could not enjoy the sacrament of Holy Communion. In a sense, we were required to "fast" from the sacrament on that day, denied by our church the body and blood, the bread and the wine, first offered by Jesus to his disciples as the sign of a new covenant of grace in the stead of the old covenant of law. The church has historically, on occasion, withheld the sacrament of Communion to keep members in line. Church law now overshadowed God's grace for us. But, as the Reformers' Wall in Geneva, Switzerland, declares in Latin, "From darkness, light." In the sermon I sought illumination in the shadow of ecclesiastical injustice.

I described the nature of sacraments in our Reformed, Protestant tradition. We recognize only two—Baptism and Communion—of the seven that many other Christians observe. In the early church, there may have been as many as 150 sacraments (e.g., the washing of feet, still practiced in some churches), affirming the sacred nature of virtually every aspect of our existence. Seven were selected by the later church to be essentially representative because the mystical number seven symbolizes completeness. Whatever the number, Christians agree that God is present in the sacraments just as God is present in the scriptures—through Jesus Christ, the Word (Logos) of God. Worship includes both word and sacrament, that is, the written and interpreted word (scripture, sermon, litany, and song), as well as the ritualized word of the sacraments (Communion and Baptism).

What is a ritual? Think how you greet the day—your own morning ritual. Alarm. Stretch. Shower. Coffee. Breakfast. Newspaper. We each have our own ways to start our mornings, our own morning rituals. Note how sensual they are: they may include sound, movement, sensation, touch, smell, taste, and vision. These rituals envelop our senses, thus incorporating or embodying all of us in the event of morning. Just as a morning ritual is a way that we greet our day with our bodies, a sacred ritual is a way that we greet

God or the holy with our bodies. But it is a two-way experience: within our morning rituals, "morning" touches us, and through the sacraments, the sacred or God touches us. A sacred ritual, or sacrament, is a *sensual* spiritual affair, reminding us that spirituality is not an out-of-body experience. As morning awakens us, a sacrament awakens us to the spiritual quality of life in a tactile and tangible way. Just as we respond to some mornings better than others, we respond to some observances of a sacrament better than others.

Our spiritual ancestors not only preserved their faith by passing on (traditioning) its spirit in words found in scripture and tradition, but also by channeling the spirit of their faith to us in rituals— specific actions that somatically engage us in the stories of faith. Scripture and tradition record both the words and sacraments to which our foreparents responded most positively.

In my second book, *Come Home!,* I wrote that word and sacrament were the two open arms with which God embraces us, welcoming lesbians and gay men home to our spiritual tradition and community after whatever estrangement we may have experienced as outcast, supposed prodigals. As I have tried to communicate this metaphor of God's welcome, I have discovered that many of us are blocked. We have experienced word and sacrament not as open hands reaching to welcome us but as spiritually abusive fists ready to pummel us, not as open arms ready to embrace us but as intimidating arms pushing us away, protectively shielding rather than openly sharing the Body of Christ, the church. Regardless of what Christians say about loving us, that Body language speaks louder than words. We do not readily experience word and sacrament as open hands reaching out and arms open wide, ready to welcome, embrace, and include us.

A sacred ritual in religious tradition is a way to relive or reenact an event wherein the sacred was revealed to our spiritual ancestors, thus revealing the sacred in our own midst. In Jewish and Christian traditions, our rituals are the means whereby we relive, remember, or reenact a redemptive event, an event in which God was present liberating, delivering, and saving us. The Jews celebrate the Passover Seder meal to commemorate their deliverance from Egyptian bondage and redemption as God's covenant community. Christians celebrate Holy Communion or the Eucharist (from the Greek word for "thanksgiving") to commemorate God's presence in Jesus Christ liberating, delivering, and saving us from the law, from sin, and from death, redeeming us for renewed community as heirs of the commonwealth of God. According to Christian tradition, all sacraments were initiated, or instituted, by Jesus during his earthly ministry as outward signs of an invisible grace. Christians believe that in Christ's very being, God "brought out" or manifested divine grace (unmerited favor). Even so, sacraments also "bring out" or manifest God's invisible grace. A sacrament serves as a means of grace, then, an objective *expression* of God's unconditional love, as well as a subjective *experience* of that love *to those who believe and participate* in those rituals.

But sacraments do more than re-present the past and represent God's grace in the present. They also serve to remind the believer of future deliverance and fulfillment in God's kingdom or commonwealth. For example, the Kiss of Peace we pass before receiving the Eucharist rarely represents a reality of a completely loving Christian community, but reminds us that mutual forgiveness is necessary in God's ultimate vision. Past, present, and future are caught up in the celebration of the sacrament.

The week of my sermon in August 1986 I had attended a stirring play about black South Africa under apartheid. It set me thinking about how funerals had become virtually sacramental for black South Africans. Under white rule their assemblies were banned; thus funerals of those martyred in the cause of self-determination became opportunities to rally the people for their mission, giving a sense of anticipated victory in the midst of present defeat, a vision of the sacred and the holy in the midst of a profane and possibly demonic political situation.

In the sermon, I considered other unconventional sacraments. Spirituals, gospel songs, jazz, and dance have surely served as revelations of the sacred for the souls of many African Americans. Civil rights marches have served as sacred events, revealing the sacred worth of a variety of minorities. The murder of Jews by the Nazi

regime prompted it to be termed a "holocaust," that is, a burnt offering, attributing sacred meaning to their deaths. Native American religions view the land and nature as sacramental and holy,
revealing spirits in what others term "inanimate" objects.

THE SACRAMENT OF COMING OUT

In light of all this, I pondered, what is the unique sacrament of
gays and lesbians?[1] Could it be sexuality? When denied access to
the standard sacraments, lovemaking serves many of us a means
of grace, a revelation of God's tender loving care. Could it be our
creativity? We have made contributions to the visual, written, and
performance arts that go far beyond our numbers in society, link-
ing us to our muse, the Creator of all. Could it be our parties? As
more than one member of our opposition has observed, we do have
better parties than most, living out Saint Irenaeus's ancient observation: "The glory of God is [a human being] fully alive."

Like black South Africans before the miraculous transformation of their nation, could funerals also be for us a sacrament in the
day of AIDS? After all, a memorial service is, for many in our
community, the only sacred act permitted us within the walls of
most churches. An AIDS funeral has often served to galvanize our
sacred resolves to help one another and exorcise this plague, thus
finding hope in the present and future.

Another possibility I considered as our unique sacrament was
ordination, because Christians willing to ordain us were doing so
defiantly, like African Americans claiming their civil rights in the
1950s and 1960s. Ordination is not a sacrament in the Reformed
tradition, as it is in others. But when it comes to our inclusion in
that rite, one might think we had all returned to our pre-Reforma-
tion roots, believing it to be so sacrosanct. My own Presbyterian

---

1. I absolutely believe in being inclusive of bisexual and transgendered people.
Throughout this book I distinguish between occasions when it feels appropriate to speak of
our common experience and rights, and occasions when I write out of gay and lesbian experience alone. There will be times when I include bisexuals and not the transgendered—
for instance, when it is a sexual matter as opposed to one of gender. In this instance, I was
speaking to gays and lesbians in the congregation.

Church had prohibited lesbian and gay Christians from ordination as ministers, elders, and deacons—thus to ordain us became an act of ecclesiastical disobedience (parallel to civil disobedience) and a sacramental inbreaking of God's grace through clouds of ignorance, legalism, and injustice. The debate over women's ordination in the Episcopal Church had led to "irregular" ordinations of women before that ban was lifted.

In our own debate over gay ordination, many supporters had suggested we argue for the opportunity of ordination based on our baptism. So in the sermon I examined the possibility that Baptism might be our sacrament, unique in the sense that we claimed it as an a priori basis for our full rights and privileges in the church. In infant baptism, most commonly practiced, we are born into the church as coheirs of the covenant of grace and as members of Christ's family long before we know our sexual identities. This position has since been argued persuasively by Marilyn Bennett Alexander and James Preston in *We Were Baptized Too*.

Still, I searched for a sacrament that we could readily claim as our own, a distinctive rite in which God was present, accessible, and experienced among us. That week I had lunch with Pat Hoffman, a close friend, writer, and fellow Christian who, though not lesbian, was someone with whom I could reflect on the question. Having visited our Wednesday night Bible study, she told me that what impressed her most deeply, what she thought was our sacrament as gay people, was our "ability to be vulnerable with one another"—in other words, experience true communion by offering our true selves. As Christ offered himself in vulnerability, so we offer ourselves, despite the risks. Being open and vulnerable may be perceived as weakness, but in reality it demonstrates our strength. By sharing our "brokenness"—how we are sacrificially cut off from the rest of Christ's Body—we offer a renewed opportunity of Communion, among ourselves and within the church as the Body of Christ. I concluded the sermon by saying that, though denied the church's Communion, we offered one another our selves as communion.

Reviewing that sermon's outline to write this book, I am stunned that I did not take the next logical step. Describing the sermon years later in workshops and retreats on the subject of this book, I added a conclusion I evidently did not make at the time: that *coming out* is our unique sacrament, a rite of vulnerability that reveals the sacred in our lives—our worth, our love, our love-making, our beloved, our community, our context of meaning, and our God.

George Chauncey has made an outstanding contribution to our understanding of recent gay American history in *Gay New York: Gender, Urban Culture, and the Making of the Gay Male World, 1890–1940*. Chauncey explains that "coming out" was first understood as a communal act, a gay version of the debutante balls in which young women were presented into society. "Coming out" before World War II introduced a gay person into gay society. At various times, coming out would come to be associated with simple self-acknowledgment, or an initial homosexual encounter, or an announcement to family and friends. It implies personal initiative, rather than the common prewar term of being "brought out," that is, by someone else's friendly initiative in private; or the more recent concept of being "outed," that is, by someone else's hostile initiative in public. Coming out was not associated with the closet in gay writings, according to Chauncey, until the 1960s. The closet became a metaphor for hiding one's sexual identity, whether from oneself, other gay people, or everyone else.

The communal nature of coming out matches the communal nature of any sacrament. "If two of you agree on earth about anything you ask, it will be done for you by [God] in heaven. For where two or three are gathered in my name, I am there among them," Jesus told his disciples in Matthew 18:19–20. By its very nature, a sacrament presupposes a community that actively participates in the ritual. Coming out is a sacrament that may be shared with one other person, a community, a congregation, a denomination, or the world.

To be complete, a sacrament anticipates the believing participation of those who are the beneficiaries. Just as the sacred nature of a sacrament cannot be forced on anyone who does not believe in its efficacy, coming out requires the cooperation and belief of those affected. This is especially true of the person who is coming out. But it is also true of other participants: a sacrament communicates the sacred, and effective communication requires giving *and* receiving. As with any sacrament, not all participants will share the same level of belief. Writing to the church at Corinth regarding the sacrament of the Lord's Supper, Paul declared, "Whoever . . . eats the bread or drinks the cup of the Lord in an unworthy manner will be answerable for the body and blood of the Lord" (1 Corinthians 11:27). Two verses later, he clarifies "unworthy" as "without discerning the body," that is, according to one view, "without discerning the community," one's relationship with other participants. Another view interprets "unworthy" to mean "without treating it as Christ's body," in other words, as sacred. Paul possibly intended both meanings, given the context of his correcting the way the sacrament was being observed in the church at Corinth.

For our purposes, we can say that those who do not welcome another's coming out receive it unworthily, without discerning either the sacred gift or their sacred kinship with the person offering her- or himself, a dissonance that may cause pain. We might also say that one may come out "unworthily," that is, for the wrong reasons, without discernment of the sacred quality of the act and of one's relationships. An example of this is the angry gay activist who decided to come out on a television talk show, notifying his family (who in turn alerted their friends in their small hometown) to watch the program—all without divulging he was gay and that that was the show's focus. One can imagine that everyone involved in that hurtful scenario suffered a diminished capacity for discerning the sacred nature of the revelation and of those relationships.

Coming out promises new life and renewed relationships just as many sacraments do. The Lazarus Project that I directed was named for the Lazarus whom Jesus called out of a closetlike tomb to new life (John 11). Jesus was deeply moved by his beloved friend's plight and by the love and faith of Lazarus's sisters, Martha and Mary—so troubled in spirit that he wept. Jesus called on Lazarus's neighbors to roll the stone from the tomb and remove the death cloths that bound him. "Come out!" Jesus cried, and Lazarus experienced not only a renewal of life but a renewal of relationship with his sisters and neighbors, as well as a fresh communion with Jesus. At their best and deepest level, sacraments renew life, relationships, community, and communion with God. At its best and deepest level, coming out means a new life, fresh and refreshed relationships, access to a new community, and increased intimacy with God.

As with most sacraments, coming out is not a singular event, but one that anticipates repetition (as Communion) or reaffirmation (as Baptism). Coming out is a lifelong process, not only because there are always new people to whom the sacred in our lives may be revealed, but also because overcoming all impediments to celebrating our "holiness" requires a lifetime (thus overcoming our own and others' homophobia and heterosexism may parallel the Christian process of sanctification—growing in grace or maturing in Christ). The church saw time as sacramental, too, baptizing already existing festivals and christening seasons as part of a Christian annual calendar that begins with Advent and Christmas and concludes with Pentecost and Christ the Sovereign Sunday, commemorating the final victory of good over evil. We also may see the sacramental nature of time as we proceed through stages of personal development in our individual coming out and of societal acceptance in our communal coming out. Just as we may mark our individual coming-out days, our community has its "high holy days" of Pride Day in June and Coming Out Day in October.

Coming out serves as a universal experience, thus a sacrament in which all are welcome to participate. Our own coming out invites others to share their secret selves, to risk intimate disclosure. Historically, many individuals and groups have come out of hiding or anonymity to declare their unique identities, understandings, beliefs, and visions. Much of this book is devoted to demonstrating how God comes out of the "closet" of heaven, revealing God's self in intimate and surprising ways, prompting people in the Bible to come out in faithful ways. Faithful lesbian, gay, bisexual, and transgendered people, as well as our families and friends and supporters, may similarly be inspired in our coming out by God's self-revelation.

Coming out bears resemblance to the seven sacraments that have become part of the broader church's tradition, while sharing particular kinship to one, which will serve as focus for this book. Those seven sacraments are Baptism, Reconciliation (confession of sins), Confirmation, Anointing of the Sick (formerly known as Last Rites or Extreme Unction), Holy Orders (religious vocation or calling), Marriage, and Holy Communion (also known as the Eucharist). In traditions that affirm a believer's baptism, as did the Baptist Church in which I was reared, Baptism and Confirmation coincide, since individual consent is a quid pro quo to Baptism. In traditions that affirm infant baptism, as does the Presbyterian Church of which I am now part, confirmation occurs at an age when the baptized are able to offer their personal assent to the Christian faith; thus they are "confirmed" in the faith of their baptism. The seven sacraments are divisible into three categories: Initiation (Baptism, Confirmation, Communion); Vocation and Commitment (Holy Orders, Marriage); and Healing and Reconciliation (Anointing of the Sick, Reconciliation).

Coming out parallels *Baptism* as we die to our old life to be raised to a new life. Baptism by immersion or sprinkling emulates Jesus' death, burial, and resurrection. As Baptism is a rite of both purification and initiation, so coming out may purify us of duplicity and compartmentalization and initiate us into a new community: that of gay, lesbian, bisexual, and transgendered people, as well as, we would hope, supportive family members and friends. We are raised to a new life of fuller integrity. It is important to distinguish integrity from perfection. We are not raised to a new life of perfection, but rather to a life of promise that we will be inspired along the path toward greater and greater integrity. Personal integrity is harmonizing who we are, what we believe, what we say, how we act, think, and feel. Spiritual integrity includes harmonizing our personal integrity with God's integrity: aligning our will with the will of God, as we discern it. It is a lifelong process that Christians call sanctification, or spiritual growth and maturation.

Coming out may serve as *Reconciliation* as we repent of the closet[2] and its myriad sinful expressions (which might include rejection of God's gift of sexuality, or involve duplicitous behavior or sexual exploitation) and offer penance by accepting God's gift of our sexuality, being honest, and seeking what Carter Heyward writes extensively about, "right relation" with others, thus reconciliation. Coming out also calls others to repent their heterosexism, offering their penance by undoing injustice. As Jesus said, "No one after lighting a lamp puts it under the bushel basket, but on the lampstand, and it gives light to all in the house. In the same way, let your light shine before others, so that they may see your good works and give glory to your [God] in heaven" (Matthew 5:15–16). Letting our light shine proves redemptive for others, reconciling us one with another, affirming our mutual ministry of reconciliation.

Coming out signals *Confirmation* in and affirmation of our creation as gay, lesbian, bisexual, or transgendered, and in our citizenship within the commonwealth of God. It serves as our personal assent to something that God has already done, that is, created us by nature and nurture, and we affirm with the psalmist: "you knit me together in my mother's womb" (Psalm

---

2. *I want to clarify this statement, which may otherwise be understood as a form of blaming the victim. I understand that the closet may be, depending on circumstance or stage of development, a necessary, healthy, and even moral choice for some at various points in time. But I believe it has implications for the person's overall health and moral well-being. The closet essentially wounds its occupant by denying her or his goodness and the quality of her or his relationships, real or potential. It interferes with communion and community, and impedes reaching out to the neighbor in need of enlightenment and the lesbian and gay neighbor in need of solidarity. Nonetheless, I also believe that coming out may be something one chooses with some and not others; discerning who is ready to receive this sacrament is crucial. But I will add that early Christians received sacraments before their significance was explained because it was believed that no one could understand their sacred nature apart from receiving them—think of the story of the travelers to Emmaus who did not recognize Jesus until he broke bread with them (Luke 24:13–35). I believe that this is also true of coming out. Sometimes beneficiaries of our coming out cannot understand its sacred import without first receiving our sacrament. I am not necessarily advocating wide public disclosure—we are not all called to make the television talk show circuit, nor follow Jehovah's Witnesses around our neighborhood, ringing doorbells. Remember Jesus' admonition against throwing pearls before swine (Matthew 7:6)! Yet I also believe we are called to a form of evangelism by availing as many as possible of the good news and sacrament we offer.*

139:13b), and "upon you I have leaned from my birth; it was you who took me from my mother's womb" (Psalm 71:6). Coming out does not answer all our questions as to why we are gay or dissolve all our doubts as to our worth, no more than confirmation in the church answers all our questions and doubts about Christian faith. But both do acknowledge "this grace in which we stand" (Romans 5:2) that is predicated not on works but on faith, according to Paul's use of the phrase. In coming out we begin to confirm our faith that we too are citizens of God's spiritual commonwealth.

Coming out offers healing, much as *Anointing of the Sick* does. This may not be readily revealed, as we sometimes witness our sacrament received with hostility and hurt. Just as anointing the sick does not cause their illness, anointing someone with our selves is not the cause of their hostility and hurt. Their hostility and hurt come from their dis-ease with homosexuality, for which we are not responsible. Just as anointing the sick may bring healing, if only by connecting those who are ill with Jesus or God or the church through the ministrations of the priest, so anointing others with our selves may bring healing of homophobia, heterosexism, and relationships broken by hiddenness, duplicity, and ignorance.

This sacrament's former rubric as "Extreme Unction" or "Last Rites" suggests another dimension of coming out, one documented in *Coming Out Within* by Craig O'Neill and Kathleen Ritter. Coming out may include coping with a kind of death, involving a grief process of letting go of certain images and possibilities and relationships, on the part of both the person coming out and the recipients of her or his sacrament. For the possibility of healing, it is best to avoid denial of whatever loss occurs, whether of vocation, of family, or of friendships.

Coming out may be viewed as a *Holy Order* of serving God, by either vocation or avocation. Simply being "out" is a form of ministry, a ministry of presence that may witness to God's inclusive love, God's creative diversity, spiritual-sexual integrity, and harmony among sexual orientations. Further, many of us, in coming out, have heard the call to render service or seek justice as volunteers or professionals. Many lesbian and gay clergy, social workers, therapists, doctors, and teachers have told me that acknowledging their own marginalization led them to want to help and empower people. From simply coming out to purposively helping others, all of these are sacred callings.

Coming out is linked to *Marriage* because both serve as a sacramental vehicle for a sacred, mutual covenant union of two lovers who promise their future love as well as the love of the moment, a covenant celebrated and supported by their assembled community. More broadly, coming out makes relationships—of whatever description—possible. A brief encounter may have value, just as a brief conversation or a fleeting friendship may have worth. A longer relationship may have greater value, just as a longer conversation or a lifelong friendship may have greater worth. Please note I use the term *may* but not *must* or the restrictive *necessarily*. We all know long-term, hurtful relationships that would have benefited by brevity. Coming out also provides opportunities for others to support lovers in their quest to love one another.

Of all the sacraments, however, I believe that coming out corresponds most closely to the sacrament of *Communion* because both involve a sacrifice and an offering that creates at-one-ment or communion with God and with others. For Christians, God is revealed in the sacrificial offering of Jesus. For our own communities, God is manifest in our own sacrificial offerings—our vulnerability and our gifts (charisms). Remember God's response to Paul regarding his thorn in the flesh? "My grace is sufficient for you, for power is made perfect in weakness," which leads Paul to conclude, "whenever I am weak, then I am strong" (2 Corinthians 12:9–10). As with Paul, our vulnerability is our strength, for therein we offer our sacred gifts of love and service. Coming out is our sacrificial offering.

Yet "sacrificial offering" conjures up undesirable images: violence, victim, martyr, and death. Is this really what God wants?

2

Sacrifices and Scapegoats

The first story of sacrificial offering in the Bible is the story of Cain and Abel (Genesis 4). Without getting into the particulars of how this story came to be, the text, as is, tells of two brothers who make their living in different ways: Cain is a "tiller of the ground" and Abel is a "keeper of sheep." Both decide to make an offering to God, apparently as a thanksgiving for what God has given them. Offering "firstfruits," returning the best of what one has been given to the God or gods who provided them, is an ancient and almost universal sacrament. But in this story, God (Yahweh) has "regard" or values Abel's gift of "the firstlings of his flock," but has no regard for Cain's gift of "the fruit of the ground." Cain becomes angry—literally, "his countenance fell." So embodied were the Hebrews that their language for emotions was characterized by states of parts of the body. God warns Cain that "sin is lurking" at his door, a predator like the Tempter in Jesus' later sojourn in the wilderness. Cain murders Abel, whose blood cries to God from the ground, and Yahweh confronts Cain, exiling him "to the land of Nod," which means "Wandering," where he and his descendants build the first city. Meanwhile, Eve bears another son, Seth, to replace Abel.

The story was told by the Hebrews to support their belief that Yahweh favored their sacrificial offerings of animals as semi-nomadic herdsfolk over those of produce from their Canaanite neighbors who were farmers. The seeming arbitrariness of God choosing to value one sacrificial offering over another is, in reality, the narcissistic reflection of the Hebrews' belief that God blessed their lifestyle rather than that of the Canaanites (though the Hebrews themselves sometimes made grain offerings alongside animal sacrifices).

Rabbinic tradition offers the concept of the midrash as a means

of explicating a scriptural text. Midrash often involves the retelling
of a biblical story in an imaginative way so that the readers may better understand its import in another context. If we were to engage in
midrash on this story to explain what it offers to our understanding
of a Bible written largely from a heterosexual perspective, the story
might go like this:

> Two brothers expressed their love in different ways: Abel was
> straight and Cain was gay. Both decide to make an offering to
> God, apparently as a thanksgiving for the sexuality that God
> has given them. God has regard for Abel's gift of heterosex-
> ual lovemaking, but has no regard for Cain's gift of homosex-
> ual lovemaking. Cain becomes angry, and God warns him that
> "sin is lurking" at his door like a predator. Cain murders Abel,
> whose blood cries to God from the ground, and Yahweh con-
> fronts Cain, exiling him "to the land of Nod," which means
> "Wandering," where he and his descendants build the first ur-
> ban gay ghetto, replete with coffee bars and antique dealers.
> Then Eve bears another straight son, Seth, to take the place of
> Abel.

Remember, this is midrash from the heterosexual perspective,
written to suggest the bias of the Bible vis-à-vis sexual orientation. I would presume that the gay or lesbian reader would
immediately see what's wrong with this picture: it is far less con-
ceivable in our experience and our understanding that the gay
brother would kill the straight brother. Rather, it is more likely
to be the other way around. The more fearful or homophobic
straight people might think it reasonable that a gay Cain could
kill a straight Abel—look how they have reacted in the United
States to the mere possibility that gay people might be admitted
to the ministry, the military, or the marriage estate! Some
straights irrationally fear that gays and lesbians are out to destroy
them and "their" institutions and "their" values. Though we
know this is not "the gay agenda," we may nevertheless gain in-
struction from this telling: we must be careful that gay rage at our
oppression does not get the better of us, causing us to respond in
sinful, violent ways.

Let's now tell the story in the opposite way:

Two brothers expressed their love in different ways. Abel was gay and Cain was straight. Both decide to make an offering to God, apparently as a thanksgiving for the sexuality that God has given them. God has regard for Abel's gift of homosexual lovemaking, but has no regard for Cain's gift of heterosexual lovemaking. Cain becomes angry, and God warns him that "sin is lurking" at his door like a predator. Cain murders Abel, whose blood cries to God from the ground, and Yahweh confronts Cain, exiling him "to the land of Nod," which means "Wandering," where he and his descendants build Straight City, replete with sports bars and suburban malls. Then Eve bears another gay son, Seth, to take the place of Abel.

This version may give us a small, somewhat vindictive laugh, but it rings of bias that few gay people would share. Most of us would not claim our sexual orientation as superior to heterosexual orientation. In other words, *we are not as biased* as our heterosexual brothers and sisters in how we regard our sexuality. Heterosexuals are more likely to accept the first midrash, in which God prefers heterosexuality, than we are to accept the second midrash, in which God prefers homosexuality.

A third midrash is needed:

Two brothers expressed their love in different ways. Abel was gay and Cain was straight. Both decide to make an offering to God, apparently as a thanksgiving for the sexuality that God has given them. God has regard for both Abel's gift of homosexual lovemaking and Cain's gift of heterosexual lovemaking. Cain becomes angry, and God warns him that "sin is lurking" at his door like a predator. Cain murders Abel, whose blood cries to God from the ground, and Yahweh confronts Cain, exiling him "to the land of Nod," which means "Wandering," where he and his descendants build Traditional Family Values Village, which outlaws gay rights. Then Eve bears another gay son, Seth, to take the place of Abel.

Now, this is more in line with how we who are gay and lesbian conceive different sexual orientations. It also reflects our experience that it is more likely for straight people to be angry at our acceptance and to bash us than the other way around.

THE SCAPEGOAT MECHANISM

The French literary critic and cultural anthropologist René Girard has, in recent decades, led a kind of cultural expedition of a wide variety of scholars into the religious psyche of human beings. He and others have argued convincingly that human language, culture, and religion emerged from "mimetic rivalry" that resulted in a "first murder," such as Cain's murder of Abel.

Mimesis is a term for the apparently innate human tendency to imitate others to create one's concept of self. We mimic other human beings in achieving our individual expressions of humanity. Girard uses the term *mimesis* because it implies acquisition: we adopt another's model or ideas (which would be "good" mimesis), or we want what they want in the sense of taking it from them ("bad" mimesis), sometimes *simply* because they want it, causing conflict. Ultimately, we come to rival those we imitate, and that rivalry forces one to eliminate the other. The "first murder," found in many cultures, refers to the original instance of such mimetic rivalry.

To explain this somewhat complex theory of civilization with a campy illustration, consider the 1950 film *All About Eve*. Eve, an ingenue played by Anne Baxter, insinuates herself into the life of a middle-aged actress named Margo Channing, delectably played by Bette Davis. Under the guise of humility, Eve learns how to act like her mentor, but—at least on the surface—without Margo's less charming qualities. Imitation is the sincerest form of flattery, yet in this case it also leads to mimetic rivalry, because Eve has cynically intended not simply to imitate but to replace Margo on stage as well as with her friends.

As I describe this movie, it occurs to me how appropriate it is that the mimetic rival here has the primordial name of Eve. If Girard is correct in his theory, mimetic rivalry goes back to the dawn of human self-awareness. Though Girard himself suggests that mimetic rivalry cannot occur between those as unequal as God and human beings, we could nonetheless consider the Adam and Eve story (Genesis 3) as a case of mimetic rivalry: both Adam and Eve ate from the forbidden tree (the tree of the knowledge of good and evil) because the serpent claimed that it would make them the equivalent of God, that is, gods. The designated "original sin," then, eating from that tree, may find its inception in our mimetic rivalry with God. (Indeed, hidden in the text may be the first instance of gender mimetic rivalry, as Adam eats from the tree to keep up with Eve, who has already done so!) Original sin may be viewed as "bad" mimesis in that it led to rivalry, a desire to possess what God alone possesses. "Good" mimesis in the garden of Eden would have caused Adam and Eve to imitate God as custodians of the garden.

According to Genesis 11, different languages were the result of another human mimetic assault on God's sovereignty, when the builders of the tower of Babel arrogantly attempted to build a tower that would reach into God's heaven, and God confused their speech, making them unintelligible to one another (Genesis 11:1–9). In the Epistle to the Romans, Paul challenged a legalistic "tower of Babel" when he claimed that justification was possible by faith in Jesus Christ alone, not by knowledge and practice of the law. The latter could be viewed as a mimetic assault on God's righteousness. Indeed, Paul's elevation of living according to the Spirit rather than the flesh (Romans 8:1–8) may be interpreted as a call to abandon *all* human attempts to assert ourselves over God, including religious ones. I have not found these specific applications of Girardian theory in the work of either Girard or his disciples, which is not to say they have not been made. But I believe that these applications reinforce this understanding of human language and culture as outgrowths of mimetic rivalry.

But, according to Girard, how does mimetic rivalry lead to a religious sensibility? I must say that I am more convinced of this second half of Girardian theory than of the first; that is, it is harder for me to conceive that all culture, language, and religion stem from mimetic rivalry, and easier to believe in what Girard describes as the "scapegoat mechanism." Mimetic rivalry leads to tensions that must be resolved. One rival must kill the other, or both must visit their tension and violence on a third party, a scapegoat. Thus ritualized violence perpetrated on a sacrificial victim reduces the likelihood and volume of other forms of violence. The sacrificial victim, devoted to God for this purpose, is thus regarded as sacred and, ambivalently, as necessarily destroyed.

In our story, Abel represents those who visit their violence on a scapegoat (in his case, firstlings of his flock) rather than a fellow human being, and God approves of this. Cain represents those who choose a fellow human being as the object of their violence, and God disapproves, nevertheless marking Cain so that the cycle of violence is interrupted (Genesis 4:15). The story of Cain and Abel thus tells us that ritualized violence is sacred—that is, "holy and acceptable" (to borrow Paul's phrase) to God, not random violence. Thus religion is born of ritualized violence in Abel's sacrificial offering of the firstlings of his flock. (Dear nonviolent reader: Do not abandon me here. We are only on the first book of the Bible; the whole story of what God wants is yet to be revealed!)

Cain's apparent sense of competition with his brother Abel reinforces Girard's concept of mimetic rivalry. God tries to put Cain's perceived "loss" in perspective by responding, "If you do well, will you not be accepted?" But that is not enough for Cain. If we look at our gay midrash of the story, the one in which both heterosexual and homosexual lovemaking are accepted on God's altar, Cain (who represents straight people in this version) is in what the Girardian school calls a "mimetic crisis." A mimetic crisis occurs when differentiation disappears, when the pecking order is no longer in place or respected. Girard offers the Plague of medieval Europe as an example of this: no matter what one's rank, both prince and pauper could be afflicted by disease. European society thereupon scapegoated the Jews, claiming they were poisoning the drinking water. To return to our third midrash, if the offerings of Cain and of Abel are equally welcome in the sight of God, differentiation fades, and this proves an intolerable situation for one who believes himself superior.

For most of my career as a gay activist, I have believed that the reason that straight society has a major problem accepting gay people, beyond sheer ignorance, is because of a fear of difference, described variously as homophobia, erotophobia, or even xenophobia. But now, in light of Girard's insights, I wonder if the opposite is also true. What if we force the dominant straight society into a mimetic crisis by asserting that we who are lesbian and gay are *just like them?* As long as we are queer, isolated in personal closets and urban ghettos, assigned (in society's mind) the most bizarre lifestyles, even "victims" of a supposed "gay" disease, there is differentiation between sexual orientations. But once we say we live in "their" neighborhoods, defend "their" countries, lead "their" churches, teach in "their" schools, live "their" lifestyles (as distinguished from whatever they believe the "homosexual lifestyle" to mean), wish to enjoy "their" institution of marriage, and warn them that AIDS is not "our" disease alone, we may be viewed like them, and they can no longer enjoy their "superior" place in the lifestyle spectrum.

In effect, we are practicing good mimesis as we follow the same sexual models and ideals as they claim to do (and as we have done throughout history), and they are practicing bad mimesis in the sense that they want to claim those models and ideals as exclusively their own. They may perceive us as mimetic rivals bent on taking away their privileges in seeking our own.

For those for whom we are still the "other" and who feel vulnerable in the perceived breakdown of "traditional family values,"[1] the scapegoat mechanism kicks in, and they, with the violence of Cain in our gay midrash, must institutionally and individually bash us to resolve the crisis. Sometimes, as required by *sacred* violence, they may even perceive us as innocent victims, "constitutional homosexuals" as the Vatican has called us, since we did not choose our sexual orientation. In his presentations and in his writings, the late Yale professor John Boswell often linked the plight of women, Jews, and gays as scapegoats in traumatic

---

1. *Complex cultural, economic, and moral issues place stress on the family of today. To believe that the desire of lesbians and gay men to establish our own family units and remain part of our biological families is responsible for the destabilization of the family is absurd, but easier to cope with than analyzing and confronting the real issues.*

times of Western civilization through the Middle Ages. In modern times, we may also see parallels with the scapegoating that involves racism, sexism, and xenophobia (practiced against immigrants who successfully claim the American dream).

Almost parenthetically I wish to add another observation related to mimetic rivalry. We in the lesbian and gay community have lamented our practice of "eating our own," that is, attacking our own leaders rather than addressing problems together—questioning their integrity, slandering their character, denouncing their competence, gossiping about their personal lives. Malcolm Boyd has called this our "crab barrel mentality" that causes us to reach up and pull down any crab that works its way to the top of the barrel. This too is a product of mimetic rivalry, for Girard explains that the scapegoat or sacrificial victim is often the king or the leader. This further explains why a nation's leaders are often unduly and unilaterally held responsible for the ills of a country. On a global scale, this accounts for unfair attacks (as opposed to fair criticisms) on the United States as a world leader.

A single explanation of sacrificial offerings, even one as intriguing as Girard's, is insufficient to account for every expression or every dimension of sacrificial offering. The ancient mind, while availing itself of much less information than we have today, nonetheless had a certain sophistication and complexity that would argue against a single explanation of any action, whether linguistic, cultural, or religious. Ancient ritual and myth themselves are so profound and enigmatic that they continue to serve us in literature, psychology, and religion. Thus to say that sacrificial offerings have a single explanation is presumptuous. I am not certain that Girard makes such a claim. I do believe that Girard's theory of the "scapegoat mechanism" is a central, even if not the only, explanation for sacrificial offerings.

SACRIFICE AS INVOCATION

Blood was life to the ancients. Flowing blood was therefore holy, sacred, divine. That is why Deuteronomic law forbad the eat-

ing of blood and required the draining of blood from an animal before being eaten (Deuteronomy 12:23–24). That is why Abel's
blood cries from the ground for God's justice—it is regarded by
God, thus holy. That is why women could not be touched during
menstruation, though the subordinate status of women and negative views of sexuality led to a misogynistic and erotophobic view
of their ritual "uncleanness" during their natural cycle.[2] Think of
the woman with the flow of blood who touched Jesus to be healed,
an action that would have rendered him ritually unclean, but which
he used to demonstrate to his listeners that the woman's faith had
made her whole (Luke 8:43–48).

Because blood was associated with divinity, the ancients believed that blood invoked God's presence. We see how the spilled
blood of the firstlings of Abel's offering brought God's attention,
as did the spilling of Abel's own blood. Bloodletting was used literally to "cut a deal," a covenant between people or between the
people and God. A covenant would be sealed in blood (think of
"blood brothers"), the sacred stuff of life, invoking God as witness.
Just as we today use words to invoke God's presence, to call for
justice, or to create a covenant, so the ancients used blood as a sacred language. They believed that the divine presence moved back
and forth between the severed parts of the body of the sacrifice in
the flow of the blood, serving as a warning to those who might vi-
olate the covenant effected (see Genesis 15:17).

Small wonder, then, that the early Christians saw in Jesus Christ's
spilled blood God's mysterious presence. I will return to the crucifixion later in this book, but for now I focus on one aspect of Christ's
crucifixion, the notion of God's demand of the sacrifice of God's
own beloved child. In this context, a scene from the film *Dominick
and Eugene* haunts me. It too is a story of two brothers, a medical
intern who serves as "his brother's keeper," a garbage collector with
a mental disability. The latter, Dominick (movingly portrayed by

---

2. In an article for Open Hands, *"Sexual Ethics in an Overpopulated World," Carol
Robb explains that blood uncontrolled by the privileged priestly class (all men, of course)
was deemed impure (vol. 13, no. 4, spring 1998).*

Tom Hulce), befriends a boy whom he later witnesses being physically abused by his father. He goes to his parish church in tears, and when a priest seeks to help him, Dominick points to Jesus on the cross and declares: "I would never let that happen to *my* son!" The film's climax renders his protest all the more poignant and ironic.

"I would never let that happen to *my* son!" We know that Jesus himself gave precedence to the family of faith and claims of the gospel over the biological family. It is ironic that traditional family values groups often consider themselves "Christian," since Jesus' own attitude flies in the face of traditional family values. He called his disciples away from their families, claiming no home for himself (Matthew 8:19–22); he proclaimed that the gospel would set family members at odds with one another (Luke 12:52–53); his "adopted" family in Bethany were all single siblings—Martha, Mary, and Lazarus; and when his own family came to visit, he declared, "Who are my mother and my brothers? . . . Whoever does the will of God is my brother and sister and mother" (Mark 3:33, 35). Despite this indifference to traditional family ties in the face of the inbreaking commonwealth of God, can we accept on a cosmic scale that God the Father and Mother would, for the sake of this commonwealth, demand the death of the Son, Jesus, to satisfy the divine sense of justice, justify the family of faith, and thus proclaim the gospel? Stay tuned.

For now, let's admit that some *human* fathers and mothers are certainly willing to sacrifice their lesbian daughters and gay sons on what they conceive as God's altar by abandoning them, which, in ancient cultures, served as a sacrifice—a figurative and often literal death sentence. Abraham thought God wanted him to sacrifice his long-awaited firstborn son, Isaac (Genesis 22:1–19). So he took Isaac to a mount, later associated with the place where the temple at Jerusalem was built (2 Chronicles 3:1), ready to sacrifice him as a burnt offering. But as Abraham prepared to spill Isaac's blood, an angel of God told him not to do it, essentially saying, in the words once used at the conclusion of the civil emergency alert checks on the radio, "This has been a test. Had this been an actual alert. . . ." And a ram is provided as a substitute.

This horrid story actually served the Hebrews as a theological advance! Just as Abel sacrificed the firstlings of his flocks, some ancient peoples, maybe even the spiritual ancestors of the Hebrews, sacrificed their firstborn children as a form of thanksgiving. This story was told to explain that Yahweh did not require this of the Hebrews and that a ram or some other animal would satisfy God as an offering of thanksgiving. The Chronicler extends the story's meaning by suggesting that the place where Abraham offered the ram in his son's stead became the site of the temple at Jerusalem, the temple whose raison d'être would be animal sacrifice.

We do not need a gay midrash of the story to see immediately how it applies to lesbians and gay men who have been cut off from their families, sacrificed on the altar of heterosexuality: thrown out, abandoned, ignored, disinherited, divorced without shared custody. Too many of our family members justify such actions on religious grounds. The concept of "tough love" is appropriated from addiction therapy as if sexual orientation falls into that category. The family is "purified" of its gay member as if Jesus had not rendered purity an immature and insufficient expression of spirituality: "Not what goes into a person is what defiles, but what comes out of a person's heart," Jesus essentially says in defense of his disciples when they do not ritually "baptize" their hands before eating (Mark 7:1–23). Jesus defends the woman of ill repute who "contaminates" the dinner party at the home of a Pharisee, ultimately telling her, "Your faith has saved you; go in peace" (Luke 7:50). Criticized for hanging out with the wrong kinds of people, Jesus quotes Hosea 6:6: "Go and learn what this means, 'I desire mercy, not sacrifice'" (Matthew 9:13). And it is the water set aside in jars for purification rites that Jesus has the audacity to transform to wine at the wedding in Cana (John 2:6). Later, Peter's vision recorded in Acts 10 would set aside for Christians the whole notion of categories defining purity, concluding that everything God has made is clean: "What God has made clean, you must not call profane" (Acts 10:15). The voice may as well have said, "What God has made sacred (i.e., everything), you must not call profane." Or, stated more positively, "All of life is a sacrament!"

SCAPEGOATING FOR ATONEMENT

The concept of purity underlies many of the reasons given for excluding lesbians and gay men from the family of faith as well. Leviticus calls a man lying with another "as a woman" ritually impure rather than morally evil (18:22; 20:13).[3] In my own Presbyterian Church, we who are gay and lesbian have been perceived as threatening the "peace, unity, and purity" of the denomination. We do not even need Girard's specific concept of mimetic crisis to see that here the supposed crisis of conflict, division, and impurity, whether in the biological family or in the family of faith, is resolved by scapegoating an expendable member.

In the body politic of the United States, the mimetic rivalry between Democrats and Republicans, no longer overcome by the real or imagined threat of communism, now visits its tensions and violence on another unifying scapegoat: the homosexual. In the midst of the political bickering, posturing, and divisiveness that characterize and paralyze our government as well as its electorate, the common sacrifice of lesbian and gay rights and the commonly held narrow-minded bigotry of heterosexism serve as atonement, at-one-ment among elected leaders of both parties and those they represent. To paraphrase the high priest Caiaphas's observation about Jesus (John 11:49–50), it is felt politically safer to abandon or sacrifice (essentially the same thing) one constituency for the sake of the nation.

To understand scapegoating, let's examine the Day of Atonement sacrifice that gives us this term (though anthropologically not the only example of such sacrifice), described in briefer and longer forms in Leviticus 16. Annually, after the chief priest sacrificed a bull to purify himself and his household, two male goats were brought forward for the sins of the people. Lots were cast to determine which would be sacrificed on the altar of God and which would be sent off into the wilderness and its demon, Azazel (mis-

---

3. Daniel Helminiak summarizes current biblical scholarship in What the Bible Really Says about Homosexuality (San Francisco: Alamo Square Press, 1994). On page 52 he points out that writers of Leviticus here could have used the Hebrew term zimah, which refers to something wrong in and of itself (a sin) but instead uses to'evah, best translated as impure or taboo.

translated "scapegoat" in the KJV, hence the term). This was not understood as a sacrifice to that demon (a demon that may be associated with the later concept of Satan, as well as the Tempter that Jesus himself faced in his forty-day fast in the wilderness). The blood of the goat on God's altar would act as a sin offering of atonement, permitting a sinful people to continue to enjoy the presence of a holy God, thus purifying the people rather than placating God. The high priest then was to "lay both his hands on the head of the [remaining] live goat, and confess over it all the iniquities of the people of Israel, and all their transgressions, all their sins, putting them on the head of the goat, and sending it away into the wilderness by means of someone designated for the task. The goat shall bear on itself all their iniquities to a barren region; and the goat shall be set free in the wilderness" (Leviticus 16:21–22). Essentially, the goat is excommunicated, exiled from the community and the communal resources for survival in the wilderness, that is, food and water and shelter. A version of the story in the Mishnah explains that the goat was pushed into a ravine; but such overt action would not have been required. Exposure without food and water would be enough for it to die, taking with it the sins of the people. (Note that Christ's crucifixion was also a form of execution by exposure.)

No great leap of our spiritual imagination is required to recognize lesbian, gay, and bisexual people in the role of these sacrificial scapegoats in today's world and today's church. We serve as scapegoats for the sins and the anxieties of erotophobia: for human guilt and suspicion regarding erotic, sensual, and sexual pleasure. After all, since homosexuality does not lead to procreation, sexuality cannot be "justified" and is experienced as an end in itself, virtually taboo in a "Christianized" if not "Christian" culture.

As those who confirm the integrity of our sexual and spiritual selves, we threaten the duality and thus the differentiation between body and spirit, sexuality and spirituality, that too long has subverted the original Jewish and Christian paradigm of soul, an indivisible unit of body and spirit that has sacred worth. We also threaten—along with many women and transgendered women and men—gender-role differentiation that is the ancient basis for much anti-gay legislation (including Leviticus 18:22 and 20:13), not to mention patriarchal and misogynistic regulation. The lack of differentiation, according to Girardian analysis, sends a culture into a mimetic crisis and sends it in search of a scapegoat, as the Jews were scapegoated for the Plague.

We similarly challenge the gulf popularly imagined between Creator and creation, the spiritual and the physical realm, when we claim our bodily and earthly experience (including our lovemaking) as a means of grace, a locus for our experience of God, an incarnation of God's tender loving care. Though both Jewish and Christian thought point also to the transcendence of God (for example, the creation story of Genesis 1), the Hebrews believed that God personally handcrafted us out of mud (the creation story of Genesis 2), tabernacled in the midst of their camp, and even wrestled with their forebear Jacob; and Christians proclaimed that God's Spirit conceived with Mary the child Emmanuel, literally, "God-With-Us," that God's Word became flesh and dwelt in our midst, thus hallowing the body through both Incarnation and Resurrection.

Yet more blatantly, we who are designated "self-affirming, practicing homosexuals" are scapegoated often by those who themselves practice sexual sin. From the twice-divorced and thrice-married U.S. representative who introduced federal anti-gay marriage legislation in Congress to the U.S. president guilty of marital infidelity who signed it into law, we see gay marriage scapegoated as the cause of the breakdown of their "traditional family values." In my own denomination, prominent male heterosexual opponents of gay ordination have met charges of multiple sexual liaisons with parishioners, incest with daughters, adultery, adultery that led to divorce, and divorce without "justifiable" cause of adultery. A commonly held opinion in the gay community that at least some of our most vociferous opponents are responding negatively to their own homosexual feelings has been vindicated by a 1997 study of self-avowed heterosexual men conducted at the University of Georgia and published in the *Journal of Abnormal Psychology*.[4]

---

4. Journal of Abnormal Psychology *105 (1996): 440–45.*

Using a gauge that measured penile arousal, 80 percent of those who were homophobic had an erotic response to a gay pornography video, while only 30 percent of nonhomophobic men did. Many self-styled "ex-gay" leaders and followers are admittedly inspired in their "change" ministries by their own debauched past and by their present shame at their ongoing sexual desires and expressions.

From the majority heterosexual perspective, it is better to scapegoat, sacrifice, and excommunicate those of us who are lesbian, gay, bisexual, and transgendered than for heterosexuals to confront their own alienation from their bodies and their sexuality, their own sexual infidelities and distortions, their own lack of spiritual-sexual integrity and certain gender identity, their own ignorance and injustice — in short, their own inability to recognize the sacramental nature of the body and of sexuality. Like the two goats of Leviticus 16, we are scapegoated in two directions. We are either cast out or our life is denied us. Using the church as an example of society at large, I will explain how this is lived out.

SPIRITUAL ABUSE

The church finally, though reluctantly, is speaking out against domestic violence and sexual abuse. But there is a form of violence and abuse that the church practices without much self-awareness and endorses with little restraint: spiritual abuse. Spiritual abuse is the wounding, shaming, and degrading of someone's spiritual worth by a perpetrator intent on taking control. Spiritual abuse is any attack (subtle or blatant, unintended or intentional) on our belovedness and sacred worth as children of God. This spiritual abuse is particularly keenly felt among gays and lesbians. Spiritual abuse is far more pervasive and permissible than other forms of abuse because it is perceived as "ordained by God." Both domestic and sexual violence are forms of spiritual abuse.[5] We can readily see the splinter of spiritual abuse in the eye of a cult, but fail to see the beam of spiritual violence and abuse in the eye of mainstream religion.

Sexual abuse or exploitation may cause its survivor to be wary of sexuality, doubtful that sexuality could be a means of communicating and receiving love. Research tells us that a victim of incest or rape may find it difficult to begin or to continue normal sexual relations. Physical abuse or exploitation may cause its survivor to wonder if the body can serve as an instrument of pleasure rather than pain. For example, a woman on a retreat explained that she had been beaten on her lower back as a child, causing her to recoil when anyone touched her there. When her new lover gave her a massage, she was terrified of what would happen when she reached the previously "forbidden" area, but found that her lover's hands proved healing and redemptive.

In similar fashion, survivors of spiritual abuse may doubt that spirituality can serve as a means of communicating and receiving love. They may be suspicious that spirituality can ever be a source of pleasure or bliss. This is the experience of many lesbians, gay men, and bisexual women and men. We are sensitive around the topic of spirituality because of the spiritual abuse we have endured. Thus we need to be reached out to with tender, loving care, like the abused woman described above. Many if not most of us have been forced outside the church, both literally and figuratively (figuratively when we remain "in" the church, but not "of" the church). Like the scapegoat sent to the demon of the wilderness, we have often been excommunicated, sent off from the "means of grace," the sacraments, denied the sustenance of the living waters of our Baptism and the nourishment of the bread and wine of Communion. It was to precisely such people that

---

5. *Part of me wants to add that* all *violence is a form of spiritual abuse. Being neither a vegetarian nor a pacifist, I can hardly assert such a belief unhypocritically (though killing plant life is also a form of violence). There is a Native American ritual of thanking the spirit of a tree or of an animal for giving up its life for the building of a canoe or the feeding of the tribe, and such a practice seems to demonstrate spiritual respect rather than abuse. But we might find little genuine spiritual respect in the ancient Hebrew practice of devoting their enemies as a sacrifice to God, or the Christian Inquisition burning witches and heretics at the stake purportedly for the salvation of their souls.*

Jesus brought the news of God's common spiritual wealth. In the context in which Jesus challenged the Pharisees to go learn what Hosea 6:6 means ("I desire mercy, not sacrifice"), he is responding to criticism that he hangs out with sinners, saying, "Those who are well have no need of a physician, but those who are sick" (Matthew 9:12). This is generally taken to mean that sinners need healing from their sin. But I believe that Jesus was explaining his mission to bring healing to those who had been spiritually abused by the Pharisees, since he makes clear in other passages that *all* are sinners, and it is the self-righteous who earn his strongest rebukes.

Those of us who have not been forced out of the church have been sacrificed on God's altar as a sin offering for other churchgoers, like the scapegoat whose blood was poured on the altar of the Israelite camp. Our lives have been taken from us, in one or more of the following ways. We have been forced to languish secretly in a closet. We have been denied intimate companionship with a partner and honest communion with others. We have been refused a livelihood in church vocation. We have been excluded from church leadership roles. We have been forced to deal almost exclusively with *this* issue, rather than enjoy the spectrum of faith and spirituality.

Finally, many of us have been sacrificed on the altar of ordination. Exodus 29 describes the sacrificial procedures to ordain the Hebrew priests, using the blood of animals for their ordination. But Exodus 32:25–29 tells quite a different story of the ordination of the sons of Levi. This tradition explains that, after the people revel and sacrifice before a golden idol, Moses comes down from Mount Sinai with great anger and dashes the tablets of the Law to pieces at the base of the mountain. He stands at the gate of the Hebrew camp and demands, "Who is on the Lord's side? Come to me!" Scripture tells us that the sons of Levi gathered around him, evidence of their faithfulness. Moses then commands them to pull out their swords and kill everyone else in the camp! After the bloody episode, Moses announces to the sons of Levi who had demonstrated their religious zeal, "Today you have ordained yourselves for the service of the LORD, each one at the cost of a son or a brother, and so have brought a blessing on yourselves this day"

(Exodus 32:29). The contrast between the ordination in Exodus 29 and that in Exodus 32 might be explained in Girardian terms: the sacrifice of a bull and a ram in the first ordination ritually avoided the murders of the second ordination. One could say that the mimetic crisis which led to the second ordination was that all the people—from the leader Aaron on down, thus no differentiation—were following one another into the sin of worshiping an idol.

In the past, I have noted that we seldom have heresy trials in the church anymore. Instead, we have trials for ordination. In these trials the church determines what is "appropriate" Christian belief and behavior. More recently, I have associated the second, bloody ordination described above with today's ordinations in churches that exclude gay people, declaring that every ordinand and every ordaining body has our blood on their hands, since ordinations do violence to those of us who are lesbian and gay, sacrificed as we are—martyred if you will—as contemporary "heretics."

Although I still like my metaphorical use of this murderous ordination, I see the broader landscape in which this irregular ordination has only a corner. While Moses is communing with the one, true, invisible God, the people demand of Aaron a visible god that they may worship. A golden calf, or young bull, is cast. It is important to note that a golden calf was a fertility god—in other words, a god of heterosexuality. Perhaps the greater metaphor in Exodus 32 is that, just as the ancient Hebrews committed idolatry by worshiping a fertility god rather than Yahweh, so Christians today have elevated their own fertility god, heterosexuality, to a place of worship that exceeds its role in creation as well as the family of faith. At the very least, one could say that many Christians certainly no longer rely solely on Christ for salvation, but rely also on their heterosexuality—an idolatrous notion in Christian thought. "Who is on the Lord's side?" Christ might ask, "Come to me!"

Are gay and lesbian and bisexual Christians thus called to put on our swords and swing through the Christian camp, eliminating heterosexist idolaters? Is all this violence really God-ordained?

3

God and Violence

Ross Greek was occasionally visited in the church office by a young man for counseling. He was attractive and gentle, had a sweet but shy disposition, and seemed—to both Ross and me—to be a closeted gay man. The reason for his visits were usually to dispel anxiety, shame, and guilt for an incident that occurred in adolescence. Like many youths with whom Ross had worked in the psychedelic '60s, this man had experimented with drugs fashionable within the counterculture. On a bad LSD trip, he hallucinated that a demon had taken over his kid sister, and he shot and killed her to exorcise the devil. Ross, who had a Ph.D. in psychology, intervened with the courts to put the young man in a drug treatment program and to work with him personally, intensively at first and later as needed. One day in January 1978, when I was out of town and Ross was out of the office, the man came by for an emergency session. Observers later said he appeared agitated and distraught. He poured gasoline all over himself in front of the church and set himself on fire. His private torment was quickly over.

How we interpret this sad final episode of this man's life may serve as a religious Rorschach test. Did he somehow pay for his original violent act with his own life? Was it a form of karmic retribution ("one who lives by the sword dies by the sword," Genesis 9:6; Matthew 26:52)? It seems like an understatement to call it a result of the "negativity" that is anathema to New Age gurus. Did it balance the scales of justice ("an eye for an eye," Exodus 21:24) or meet the death sentence for murder required after the flood (Genesis 9:6)? Could it have served as a contemporary expression of propitiation (appeasement) or expiation (reparation) for his sin to God or the gods, a sacrifice as ancient as human civilization? Was it a penitential act, a sacrifice crying for mercy?

Or was it simply another violent act that had only *intended* or *perceived,* rather than *actual,* significance, other than to grieve the hearts of those who loved him and to grieve the heart of God who both loves him and abhors all violence? (The present tense of "loves him" here is intentional, as I believe that God's love never ends and eternally upholds us.)

At an earlier time in my Christian faith I would have wanted to tell the young man that it was only necessary for one to die, and that, in the crucifixion of Jesus Christ, he was forgiven, no matter what he had done. Now I am inclined to say that Jesus' crucifixion itself was simply another violent act that had only perceived, rather than actual, significance, other than to grieve the hearts of those who loved him and love him and to grieve the heart of God who both loves him and abhors all violence.

To state my feeling as plainly as that fills me with apprehension. It contradicts much of what I have been taught. And doesn't it fly in the face of all Christian tradition? (This is a question I will address later.) Yet no one took me to task when I wrote essentially the same thing ten years ago in my autobiography, *Uncommon Calling*—that I believed it was the will of *humanity* that Jesus die; that the will *of God* was revealed in the Resurrection. In my second book, *Come Home!*, I wrote of letting go of a notion of an all-powerful God in favor of the concept of an all-loving God, since logic argues that God cannot be both. To choose love over power, I used the argument of friendship: are the people that you hold dear loved by you because they are powerful or because they are loving? Yet then I went beyond even that line of reasoning, because I had come to realize that human conceptions of power are distorted—that indeed, *God's power is love*. God's power is persuasive, not coercive; God is the Good Shepherd, not the benevolent control freak. In the Bible, God was viewed as king or sovereign, but in an ideal sense—God as a shepherd-king, like David. True and absolute and holy power is love, not control. Love "does not insist on its own way" but "rejoices in the truth. It bears all things, believes all things, hopes all things, endures all things" (1 Corinthians 13:5–7). Finally, "God is love" (1 John 4:8).

Admittedly, Christianity is based on a foundational belief that Jesus Christ was sacrificed as an expiation for our sins, as Paul interpreted the Christian story in a way not explicit in the Synoptic Gospels of Matthew, Mark, and Luke (though represented in the chronologically later Gospel of John). I might view myself as "pre-Christian," understanding my faith to originate in the person of Jesus himself, rather than the sacrificial layers that have buried him once more, but such self-designation seems both smug and pointless. Even those who believe that Jesus' death had cosmic significance recognize that the crucifixion would have had little meaning without his teachings. Some biblical scholars believe that the commissioning of the seventy disciples in Luke 10 may allude to a "Jesus movement" that preceded the Passion (that is, the final sacrifice of Jesus' life), in which disciples carried Jesus' teachings throughout Palestine without the impetus of the Passion narrative. Thus the salvific effects of Jesus' life precede whatever saving role the cross played. The Gospels themselves tell us that Jesus' very presence and touch and voice offered forgiveness of sins, healing of bodies, and even resurrection from death—all to those who believed—and all of these transformations preceded the final week of the Passion. In Jesus, the kingdom or commonwealth of God had come near long before either crucifixion or resurrection.

In the Gospels the space devoted to Jesus' death was more likely intended to serve as an apologia for how a God-sent Messiah could suffer and die by a criminal's execution (especially under the onus of "anyone hung on a tree is under God's curse," Deuteronomy 21:22) than to place undue emphasis on the salvific significance of Jesus' death apart from his life and resurrection. The earliest church teachers ("Fathers") affirmed the atoning effect of Jesus Christ's totality—life, death, and resurrection—without singling out the crucifixion as the only or primary event necessary for our salvation from the effects of the law: sin and death. (I must add here that the early church teachers believed that the life, death, and resurrection of Christ had an objective, not simply a perceived, reality.) Only later, in the Middle Ages, did a culture wracked by plague, famine, war, and poverty lead to the suffering and death of Christ taking center stage in the spiritual imagination of the church.

I can illustrate this point by yet another reference to a film. Especially in the gay and lesbian community, we are more likely to attend films than worship. Films may serve as contemporary sermons, sometimes "bad" in the sense of being preachy, didactic, simplistic, ill-researched, badly written, or poorly delivered, but sometimes "good" in the way they capture our spiritual imagination and highlight spiritual truths, like biblical storytelling and Jesus' own parables. The recent film *Breaking the Waves* was that kind of film for many; but whether it achieved such a goal has sharply divided critics and moviegoers. I saw the film with my lover and a Lutheran pastor shortly after its release. My often skeptical lover was deeply moved by the film. I, who can be moved to tears by a poignant television commercial or a charitable act reported on the news, did not share his innocent wonder at the movie. Both the Lutheran pastor and I were disturbed by it.

The protagonist of *Breaking the Waves* is a young woman with an apparent mental disability who lives in a remote coastal village along the North Sea. The religion practiced there is austere, symbolized by the village church having no bell. She is the custodian of the church and has conversations with God in which she plays both parts, taking on a stern, fatherlike-from-above tone when assuming the role of God. Her God is not altogether ungracious, but is nevertheless demanding. Shortly after her marriage, her husband is immobilized by an accident on an offshore oil platform, and his illness causes him to urge his wife to have sexual affairs with men and describe them to him—thus to enjoy her vicariously. Everyone in the village unknowingly reinforces his proposal by insisting that she support her husband regardless, ignorant of the nature of his requests. So she sacrifices herself sexually, offering herself up to social, sexual, and physical abuse because she believes her actions to be the will of God. Indeed, her ultimate sacrifice brings about two miracles that the filmmakers must have intended to instill compassion and awe in the moviegoer.

I was troubled by the movie because, though I wished otherwise, I felt the protagonist to be pathetic rather than someone with whom I could adequately identify and be sympathetic. I understand why feminists could see the film infused with a misogynistic light in that, once again, a woman is sacrificed for a man's redemption. But the larger picture is what really grabbed and twisted my entrails: the seemingly required association of violent sacrifice with God's intervention.[1]

I do believe that when our ancient spiritual ancestors experienced the presence of God in the shedding of blood of either a human or animal sacrifice, they were on to something. I believe that God was there, but not for the reasons they supposed. (I am aware of my presumption of their reasons.) I believe that God was there not because God delighted in this method of giving thanks, not even because God delighted that human beings were channeling their violence ritually rather than randomly, but because God was there between the severed pieces of the broken animal *trying to bring those pieces back together,* to heal the breach, to reconcile the parts, to stop the sacred flow of vitality that we call blood. God was there willing at-one-ment for what human beings separated; God was there choosing life for the sacrificial victim. From my Christian perspective, God the Creator of life and the Author of love could hardly be satisfactorily viewed as either demanding death or requiring violence.

Yes, some passages in the Bible seem to justify the conception of the Old Testament God as a God of wrath and violence, like the destruction of Sodom and Gomorrah by fire and brimstone, the ten plagues of Egypt (especially the final plague causing the death of all firstborn sons of Egypt), the "holocaust" of Jericho that God "required" when the Israelites lay claim to the land of Canaan, as well as their whole "God-endorsed" conquest of the Canaanites, and the destruction of enemies often called for by the psalmists. But these passages could also be understood as ancient attempts to explain natural phenomena, to justify human violence and national interest (as in "holy" war), or to vent anger. A very different God

---

1. *Feminist, womanist, and mujerista theologians have challenged the association of God and violence. Though I believe the reasons for their challenge are valid, I have chosen to take a different tack than applying a specifically feminist ideology or theology to the question. Christian feminists have revealed that the Bible provides basis enough to question the "sacred" nature of violence.*

eventually emerges from the shadows of the closet labeled "Hebrew national deity."

In the New Testament, the sword serves merely as metaphor in a saying of Jesus (Matthew 10:34), in the writings of Paul (who includes "the whole armor of God" in Ephesians 6:11–17), and in Hebrews 4:12. The book of Revelation, a problematic text for many reasons, uses violent imagery in a vision of violence finally subdued by the *Lamb* of God—once again, implying the use of violence as metaphor.

GOD REJECTS VIOLENCE

In the majority of the stories and texts of the Bible, I believe that God comes out as one who rejects violence, sacred or otherwise. When the first verses of the Bible depict Yahweh's creation of the cosmos, the Hebrew God does so by creativity, not by violence, as was common in other ancient myths of creation. The garden of Eden, the paradigm for life on earth, was by nature nonviolent, since Adam and Eve were apparently vegetarians and offered no sacrifices to enjoy communion with God in their evening walks. God does not even respond with violence when Adam and Eve sin, though increasing childbirth pain (Genesis 3:16) and driving them from the garden and the tree of eternal life (3:22–24) may be seen as bloodless forms of violence (as well as simple folklore on the origins of birth pangs and of death). Even so, the God of Eden behaves mildly compared to the deities of many other world-founding myths.

In response to the first human murder, God, though attentive to Abel's blood crying from the ground, marks the murderer Cain so that no one will do violence to him to repay his own violence. What we might view as a natural disaster, the flood, the ancients understood as an act of God destroying the wicked. Yet the central story is that of God saving human and animal life aboard the ark, and immediately afterward, setting a bow in the clouds as a sign of a covenant never to resort to this kind of violence again. A horizontal bow in an age of bows and arrows meant God's unilateral disarmament: God laid down a weapon of violence.

God would later deliver the Hebrews from the violence of slavery in Egypt and create Ten Commandments to prevent violence among the people. God limited retributive violence with the rule, "If any harm follows, then you shall give life for life, eye for eye, tooth for tooth, hand for hand, foot for foot, burn for burn, wound for wound, stripe for stripe" (Exodus 21:23–25). This, in effect, served as a restraining order to prevent the cycle of vengeful violence from escalating—that is, causing greater harm in avenging the original injury, harm that would require yet another violent rejoinder in a never-ending cycle of violence (feuds).

The prophet Jeremiah pointed out that sacrifice was not required during the days of wandering in the wilderness (Jeremiah 7:22). There God tabernacled with the people, leading them finally to a promised land of milk and honey, peace, health, and prosperity. Later, God was with them in the Babylonian exile and restored them to Jerusalem.

GOD SUBVERTS VIOLENCE

As a subversion of violence, both the Bible and the God it reveals side with the victims of violence, sacrifice, and scapegoating, as Girard and an interpreter, James Williams, point out (see the bibliography). God heard the cries of the Hebrews in Egypt and intervened to remove their victimization. "I have observed the misery of my people who are in Egypt; I have heard their cry on account of their taskmasters. Indeed, I know their sufferings, and I have come down to deliver them from the Egyptians, and to bring them up out of that land to a good and broad land, a land flowing with milk and honey," Yahweh told Moses from the bush that burned without being consumed (Exodus 3:7–8). The symbolic representation of God itself is nonviolent, in that the bush is not devoured by the flame of God.

Many of the Psalms were written from the perspective of victims. "More in number than the hairs of my head are those who hate me without cause," the psalmist lamented; "I have become a stranger to my kindred, an alien to my mother's children" (Psalm

69:4, 8). Recently I heard a woman read this psalm as an opening meditation for a clandestine gay, lesbian, and bisexual support group on a seminary campus. "I never understood what it was like to have what the psalmist calls 'enemies,'" she admitted, "until I came out as a lesbian in the church." The psalmist continues in the same psalm with a theme repeatedly acknowledged in other psalms that God is on the side of victims:

> I will praise the name of God with a song;
> I will magnify [God] with thanksgiving.
> This will please the LORD more than an ox
> or a bull with horns and hoofs.
> Let the oppressed see it and be glad;
> you who seek God, let your hearts revive.
> For the LORD hears the needy,
> and does not despise [God's] own that are in bonds.
> (Psalm 69:30–33)

The psalmist declares that God prefers a song of thanksgiving to a sacrifice of an animal, since God is on the side of all victims, all of the oppressed.

Job, a victim paradigm, gave voice to all who have suffered unjustly, challenged being scapegoated by his religious friends, and unashamedly confronted God. He himself had demonstrated his righteousness by championing the victim:

> I delivered the poor who cried,
> and the orphan who had no helper.
> The blessing of the wretched came upon me,
> and I caused the widow's heart to sing for joy.
> I put on righteousness, and it clothed me;
> my justice was like a robe and a turban.
> I was eyes to the blind,
> and feet to the lame.
> I was a father to the needy,
> and I championed the cause of the stranger.
> (Job 29:12–16)

The book of Esther is written from the perspective of an intended victim, the Hebrews, and a potential victim, Esther. When a pogrom is to be executed against her people, Esther requested that they join her in fasting as she shrewdly and courageously risks her life to avoid their victimization. The book of Ruth is written from the perspective of economic victims, as Ruth and Naomi cleverly and lovingly work together to ensure their survival in a society with limited economic opportunities for women and one that encouraged their dependency on men. We will look more closely at the stories of Esther and of Ruth and Naomi in chapter 4.

The prophets themselves sided with the victims of violence, stating most clearly God's preference for justice and mercy rather than sacrifice. Living on the margins of society, sent out by God in much the same way that the scapegoat was excommunicated by the high priest, the prophets identified with the marginalized, the victims, the scapegoats of Israelite society. As Isaiah writes in his first chapter:

> Hear the word of the LORD,
>   you rulers of Sodom!
> Listen to the teaching of our God,
>   you people of Gomorrah!
> What to me is the multitude of your sacrifices?
>   says the LORD;
> I have had enough of burnt offerings of rams
>   and the fat of fed beasts;
> I do not delight in the blood of bulls,
>   or of lambs, or of goats. . . .
> When you stretch out your hands,
>   I will hide my eyes from you;
> even though you make many prayers,
>   I will not listen;
>   your hands are full of blood.
> Wash yourselves; make yourselves clean;
>   remove the evil of your doings
>   from before my eyes;
> cease to do evil,

learn to do good;
seek justice,
rescue the oppressed,
defend the orphan,
plead for the widow.
(Isaiah 1:10–11, 15–17)

Of particular interest to us is that Sodom and Gomorrah, mistakenly associated in modern times with homosexuality, are here associated with sacrifice. Their sin was that they believed that God wanted sacrifices rather than justice for the oppressed. This neatly fits into the interpretation, implied by the prophet Ezekiel ("Sodom . . . did not aid the poor and needy," Ezekiel 16:49) and assumed by Jesus (Matthew 10:14–15; Luke 10:11–12), that Sodom and Gomorrah were destroyed for their inhospitality to the marginalized (the poor and the stranger). The men of Sodom wanted to sacrifice the strangers in Lot's house by victimizing them with gang rape, a familiar ancient practice by which straight men humiliated other men. Their inhospitality was just another form of scapegoating.

Of course Isaiah was not literally addressing Sodom and Gomorrah, which were long since gone. Isaiah was connecting his religious community with those infamous cities, thus equating their sins just as Jesus would do later when he sent his disciples throughout the countryside and said that if they are not welcomed in any village, "It will be more tolerable for Sodom than for that town" (Matthew 10:12). We may equate the sins of Sodom and Gomorrah with our own religious communities that wish to humiliate us, victimizing us with spiritual rape and sacrificing us as scapegoats.

Hosea, Amos, and Micah share convictions similar to Isaiah's. Could not Hosea be rebuking loveless churches that reject our own steadfast love, sacrificing us on their altar of ritual "purity," when he speaks for God: "For I desire steadfast love and not sacrifice, the knowledge of God rather than burnt offerings" (Hosea 6:6, quoted by Jesus in Matthew 9:13 and 12:7)? Through Amos, God admonished:

I hate, I despise your festivals,
　　and I take no delight in your solemn assemblies.
Even though you offer me your burnt offerings and grain
　　offerings,
　　I will not accept them;
and the offerings of well-being of your fatted animals
　　I will not look upon.
Take away from me the noise of your songs;
　　I will not listen to the melody of your harps.
But let justice roll down like waters,
　　and righteousness like an ever-flowing stream.
                                                                (Amos 5:22–24)

God prefers justice for the victims of injustice over worship—no
matter how glorious and pure—in which victims are sacrificed.
God prefers justice for us rather than worship from the churches
that sacrifice us on their altars.

　　Micah also contrasted sacrifice with God's requirements:

"With what shall I come before the LORD,
　　and bow myself before God on high?
Shall I come before [God] with burnt offerings,
　　with calves a year old?
Will the LORD be pleased with thousands of rams,
　　with ten thousands of rivers of oil?
Shall I give my firstborn for my transgression,
　　the fruit of my body for the sin of my soul?"
[God] has told you, O mortal, what is good;
　　and what does the LORD require of you
but to do justice, and to love kindness,
　　and to walk humbly with your God?
                                                                (Micah 6:6–8)

Again, justice, mercy, and humility are called for, not the peace,
unity, and purity that institutional religion seeks by sacrificing
scapegoats such as ourselves.

　　What biblical scholars refer to as Second Isaiah (Isaiah 40–66),
written after Isaiah's lifetime, brings the prophetic insight of God's

siding with the victim to its ultimate conclusion in the image of the
Suffering Servant, which may be viewed as the witness of the nation
of Israel to the world, or as a foreshadowing of a Messiah who would
redeem Israel and the world, or as both. In any case, God is manifest in the suffering of this victim, whose very innocence cries out
for a stop to sacrifice:

> He was despised and rejected by others;
> > a man of suffering and acquainted with infirmity;
> and as one from whom others hide their faces
> > he was despised, and we held him of no account.
> Surely he has borne our infirmities
> > and carried our diseases;
> yet we accounted him stricken,
> > struck down by God, and afflicted.
> But he was wounded for our transgressions,
> > crushed for our iniquities;
> upon him was the punishment that made us whole,
> > and by his bruises we are healed.
> > > > (Isaiah 53:3–5, fourth Servant Song)

Admittedly, ambiguity surrounds God's will regarding the Suffering Servant in the Isaiah text. On the one hand, "by a perversion of
justice he was taken away" (53:8), but on the other, "the LORD has
laid on him the iniquity of us all" (53:6). This uncertainty reflects,
I believe, human and especially Jewish ambivalence toward the notion of sacrifice: it may be felt necessary, though not God's druthers.
Yet now we finally have the perspective of the innocent victim of
sacrifice. Sacrificial animals do not speak, for they are "like a lamb
that is led to the slaughter, and like a sheep that before its shearers
is silent" (53:7, fourth Servant Song), but now through Isaiah "The
LORD God has given me the tongue of a teacher" (50:4, third Servant Song). The reader's compassion is called out, thereby joining
God in despising at least the need for sacrifice if not sacrifice itself,
and identifying true worship as release of the intended victim:

> Is not this the fast that I choose:
> > to loose the bonds of injustice,

> to undo the thongs of the yoke,
> to let the oppressed go free,
> and to break every yoke?
> (Isaiah 58:6)

Long before we come to Christian scriptures, God comes out in Jewish scriptures as one who opposes violence even for religious or sacred purposes.

GOD COMES OUT

A central tenet of Reformed faith, which harks back to Augustine, is the concept that God is known to us by revelation—that is, by divine rather than human will. God can neither be "brought out" nor "outed" no matter how well-intentioned our human motives may be. No biblical writer, no religious figure, no mystic, no scholar, no priest, no preacher, no teacher, and no reader of the Bible may know God unless God makes Godself known to them. This need not be a cause for despair to those who want to know God, because God willingly, eagerly, and repeatedly comes out to God's creatures, even apart from the Bible. In Romans 1 Paul points out that "ever since the creation of the world [God's] eternal power and divine nature, invisible though they are, have been understood and seen through the things [God] has made" (Romans 1:20).

But the awesome, fearsome nature of God makes us want to cover our eyes when confronting God's revelation of self. Moses could not see God's face and live, and the glow of his face from viewing God's mere rear was so overwhelming that the people prevailed upon him to cover his face (Exodus 33:18–33; 34:29–35). This seems to justify C. G. Jung's characterization of religion as our defense against the experience of God. Almost by definition, religion is compelled to closet God, for it provides a comparatively safe means by which to come near to God, whose unitive essence threatens our categories, our assumptions, our sense of differentiation and of power. As originally understood and practiced, the sacrificial system, though intended to invoke or assure God's presence, served and still serves (in a ritualized form in the Eucharist viewed as reenacting the sacrifice of Christ and in a more direct form in scapegoating victims) as a primary way by which we avoid God's self-disclosure, at least in the context of religious practice. Violence—even ritualized—does not attract real intimacy with anyone, let alone a nonviolent God. How is it that we, who are only able to see "in a mirror, dimly" (1 Corinthians 13:12), have the veil of Moses removed so that "all of us, with unveiled faces, seeing the glory of the Lord as though re-flected in a mirror, are being transformed into the same image from one degree of glory to another" (2 Corinthians 3:18)?

The God who reveals Godself throughout the pages of the Bible calls upon all of us to remove our veils, to come out in countless ways, through the stories of people of faith. As the author of Psalm 139 declared, even though God has searched us and known us and there is no place to flee from God's presence, we still either try to hide or, at times, feel hidden from God. Before considering further God's coming out in the Bible, let's review the coming-out stories of a representative sampling of our biblical ancestors that may illu-mine dimensions of our own coming out. Just as self-disclosure en-ables lesbian, gay, bisexual, and transgendered people to find one another, so our own coming out opens us to God's self-revelation.

4

Coming Out in the Bible

Coming out is a theme in scripture in a way that homosexuality is not. The latter has as few as five debatable references. But coming out is a recurring if not central theme of the Bible, easily recognizable to those familiar with the experience and process of coming out as lesbian, gay, bisexual, transgendered, or as family, friend, or advocate of someone who is. This links our own experience with that of our spiritual ancestors as well as opens us up to the universality of the life-giving and life-changing coming-out process for every human being. Just as coming out to God opens up the chosen or called in the Bible to God's own coming out, so our vulnerability creates a welcome sanctuary for God's self-disclosure. "To the humble [God] shows favor" (Proverbs 3:34), and God "teaches the humble [God's] way" (Psalm 25:9).

The coming out of our biblical forebears may serve as a mythological means to illumine our own coming out. In religious tradition, a myth is not a story that is not true, but a story that carries deeper meaning than may be literally present or even possible. Some particulars of the story may have shifted in its retelling, but, as with a sacrament, the sacred is revealed in the process of its telling—in the story's own coming-out process. Because I have faith in this process, I reflect on the following biblical tales with little or no assessment as to their probability. Though I am rigorous in my own writings to tell the truth as far as I am able in recounting personal stories, I do not demand this of scripture, for what ultimately matters is a story's meaning for the people of faith of its time, of history, and of the present.

In other words, in this chapter, I accept the biblical accounts pretty much at face value—or rather, at faith value. I am not a literalist, but my understanding of biblical authority requires me to find the meaning of the biblical story for our faith today, through the help of the Holy Spirit; through God-given reason and imagination and love; through Jesus Christ who has made me, as a Christian, an heir to the spiritual wealth therein; and through the church tradition and scholarship that has molded me and my faithful inquiry.

I have already introduced my hermeneutic—that is, my method for re-viewing (not revisioning) scripture: coming out. Through the theme of coming out, I will revisit biblical stories familiar to most readers, rather than using obscure passages.

In *The Gates of the Forest,* Elie Wiesel tells the story of a rabbi who averted a disaster for his people by meditating at a certain spot in the forest, lighting a fire, and offering a prayer. The next time catastrophe approached, one of his disciples went to the same site, offered the prayer, but did not know how to light the fire—and still miraculously avoided disaster. Later, another rabbi went to the sacred spot, but knew neither the prayer nor how to light the fire; yet it was enough to save his people. Finally, another rabbi, in a similar desperate situation, knew neither the prayer, the fire, nor the place, but he could tell the story, and that retelling again prevented calamity.[1] The Bible is filled with stories like that, the simple telling of which may deliver us from hopeless adversity.

Wiesel concludes, "God made [human beings] because he loves stories." That means our stories as well.

COMING OUT
OF INNOCENCE AND SHAME

The idyllic innocence of the garden of Eden depicted in the opening chapters of Genesis would appear to render coming out unnecessary. Duplicity, secrecy, and closets would seem superfluous in an environment of creaturely harmony and regular, intimate communion with God. Yet central to this perfect environment, in the middle of the garden, there was a tree closeted behind a taboo: God forbad Adam and Eve from eating of the tree of the knowledge of good and evil. Newly created, as the story goes, Eve and Adam would be virtual children. We know how curious children

---

1. *Elie Wiesel,* The Gates of the Forest *(New York: Holt, Rinehart & Winston, 1966).*

are, especially when told not to do something. Children—especially the first—know little of death and feel invincible, so Adam and Eve would not have understood the warning that they would die if they ate of the tree. Even without the duplicitous serpent, Adam and Eve were likely tempted by the tree's tantalizing forbiddenness. When the serpent explained that it held the secret of becoming like God, they ate. Immediately they realized they were naked and felt shame at their bodies. They hid behind trees when God came to walk with them in the cool of the day, ashamed of their nudity as well as their sin. God called them out of the very first closet to inquire what had interfered with their communion.

A friend of mine told me that, as a teenager growing up in a small town in New England, he and his boyfriend discovered each other's bodies. They found themselves pleasuring one another, loving one another, without the slightest hint in their minds that they might be doing something "wrong." After they discovered a wonderful plant to rub *all over* each other's bodies, the village doctor who treated them both for poison ivy never breathed a word that their intimacy was forbidden. In their Boy Scout troop, same-sex exploration was playful and innocent, without the intrusion of adult exploitation or judgment. Only when a teacher was run out of town for being a homosexual did all their activity come to an abrupt halt. They never spoke of what had gone on before the "knowledge of good and evil." My friend, who was gay, submerged his natural feelings deep within a psychic closet sealed with shame.

Those with same-gender attractions are not the only ones likely to be taught shame regarding our bodies and our sexuality: this is a fairly common experience among heterosexuals as well. "Who told you that you were naked?" God asked of Adam and Eve (Genesis 3:11). Who told us that we were naked? Who told us that we should be ashamed of our bodies and of our sexuality? Who told us to hide our nakedness and our sexuality? Not the Creator in the garden of Eden who wishes to walk daily with us, in mutual self-disclosure, "at the time of the evening breeze" (Genesis 3:8). With Eve and Adam, God beckons us to come out from behind the trees that we hope will hide our bodies and our sexuality.

Our physical creation is our original blessing; our sexuality is our sacred pleasure.

COMING OUT AS DREAMERS

Joseph (whose story appears in Genesis 37, 39–50) was far from the firstborn of his family, so he could expect little, if any, inheritance. Yet he was the first son of Jacob's true love, Rachel, whose older sister, Leah, Jacob had been tricked into marrying first. Rachel had tragically died in the birth of Benjamin, their other son. So Jacob had a special love for Joseph that angered his brothers, and they resented Jacob's gift to him of a very special robe, which tradition has called a "coat of many colors." It may have simply been a robe with long sleeves, intended for royalty and not for work, the latter requiring sleeveless and shorter tunics. Second Samuel 13:18 confirms the association with royalty by explaining that King David's *daughters* wore such garments. (Cross-dressers take heart!?)

No wonder that Joseph felt encouraged to come out about his dreams, dreams that he was special and that his own family would come to honor him. Jacob himself rebuked his son for such dreams, but he pondered them. After all, he too had been visited by God in dreams that revealed his identity and his destiny, dreams that set him at odds with his own brother, Esau.

Jealous of the blessings that God apparently bestowed on Joseph, his brothers plotted to kill him as he approached them in pasturelands far from home. "'Here comes this dreamer,' they said to one another. 'Come now, let us kill him and throw him into one of the pits; then we shall say that a wild beast devoured him, and we shall see what becomes of his dreams'" (Genesis 37:19–20).

But Reuben, the eldest of the brothers, wanting to avoid both bloodshed and guilt, suggested another option: throwing Joseph into a cistern without killing him. He would not want his brother's blood crying for vengeance from the ground, as Abel's blood had done. The story claims that Reuben intended to rescue him later.

Joseph was stripped of his royal garment and thrown into the cistern. What happened next probably reflects the blending of two separate accounts. Judah suggested selling Joseph into slavery behind Reuben's back. The brothers eagerly agreed. Joseph was sold for twenty pieces of silver, reminiscent to modern hearers of the story of the thirty pieces of silver for which Judas would later betray another dreamer, Jesus.

The brothers were rid of Joseph, but, as it turned out, only for the time being. Little did they know at the time the role they had played in God's providence, for they had delivered him into the hands of those who would take him to Egypt, where his dreams would come true. Joseph's vocation of dreams inspired his interpretation of Pharaoh's dream portending a famine, and Joseph would later be placed in a position to help the very brothers who had wanted to do away with him, providing them with the stored grain that saved them from a famine and made familial reconciliation possible. They would indeed come to value him.

That is the dream of many of us whom mainstream churches have labeled "self-affirming," "avowed," "practicing," and "unrepentant" homosexuals. Just as Joseph did, we have come out as self-affirming, avowed, practicing, and unrepentant *dreamers,* who dream of finding both ministry and reconciliation within our families of faith. The first religious story that I wrote as a child was a retelling of Joseph's story. I already felt "queer"—different from others, misunderstood. Yet I also had a sense that I had something valuable to offer my family and my family of faith. I dreamed of a tearful reconciliation before I fully understood the nature of the alienation. I dreamed of saving others before I knew what deliverance was needed.

Joseph's family story offers clues to the church's story as the family of faith in how the church deals with self-affirming, practicing dreamers (saints, if you will) who are not quite cut from the same mold and yet who come out to serve God's purpose in a unique way among the *ekklesia*—the Greek word for "church" that literally means those *called out*—as we parallel in faith the chosen quality of Jacob and Rachel's lineage. Just as Joseph had little hereditary claim because of his birth order, we dreamers would appear to have no claim by virtue of our gender, color, sexual orientation, or disability.

Yet we have dreams that trouble those who lay claim to the church's inheritance. We have dreams that we too may be ordained, serve as pastors and lay leaders, lead governing bodies.

Then there are the siblings—brothers and sisters in Christ who are jealous of the dreamers and see no reason why our lives or our relationships should be blessed. If they had their druthers, they would kill the dreamers who rattle the church as institution. But, doing things with decency and order, they are open to a more civilized alternative. Reubens in the church offer this alternative. "The Reuben Option," as the Reverend Allan Boesak of South Africa has named it, is to put dreamers away where they cannot be seen. Invisible, they are left to languish in dry cisterns, in closets, sometimes in specialized ministries. Then there is what I call "the Judah Option": selling dreamers into ecclesiastical slavery. Put them on committees, let them endure bureaucratic drudgery, use them as tokens, but never really listen to their dreams for the church and the world. Invite them to become members of the church, welcome their gifts, but do not allow them in ordained leadership.

The Reuben and Judah options allow the church to attain a semblance of peace, unity, and purity. But this means sacrificing and scapegoating the Josephs in the church family, those with large dreams and divine callings. For the sake of the peace, unity, and purity of the family, the church says, let's put Joseph down an empty cistern and sell him into slavery. Avowed, practicing dreamers are a nuisance. What right do they have to believe they might have any authority in our family? Why should they be given a royal robe of many colors and long sleeves, or a clerical robe? Why should they be given a blessing?

Lesbians and gay men and bisexuals and the transgendered are in good company—a cloud of self-affirming, practicing dreamers. We share with Joseph the feeling of destiny, of being called to some unique task. We share with Joseph not a multicolored coat but a multicolored banner, our rainbow flag that celebrates our diversity while claiming the sacred promise of the rainbow. As the Reformers would have it, we are all uniquely called to serve. Perhaps those of us who are not likely to achieve "success" in our own lifetimes are more likely to be aware that we are dreamers. But we *all* have our dreams. The spiritual life is a way to access our dreams and to come out as dreamers.

"Then we shall see what becomes of his dreams," Joseph's brothers had said. We know that his dreams came true, and that his vision saved not only him but his family. It is our dreams that give those marginalized by the church the faith that, though cast into a pit or sold into slavery, God will bless us as we bring reconciliation within our families of faith and save the church from its famine of dreams.

COMING OUT OF OPPRESSION

Joseph's dream eventually turned into a nightmare for his people. As Exodus tells it, after Joseph's death, a pharaoh came to power in Egypt who forgot the debt to Joseph and his people that had arisen because Joseph had interpreted Pharaoh's dream to mean famine and led Egypt in preparing for it and surviving it. Feeling threatened by the numbers and power of the Hebrews, Pharaoh decided to enslave them. "But the more they were oppressed, the more they multiplied and spread, so that the Egyptians came to dread the Israelites" (Exodus 1:12). Feeling more threatened, Pharaoh ordered the midwives of the Hebrew women to kill every male baby. But scripture says that "the midwives feared God" (Exodus 1:17) and let the babies live, explaining to Pharaoh that the Hebrew women were so strong they delivered before the midwives arrived.

That's why Moses' mother placed him in a basket and hid it in the reeds of the river. There Pharaoh's daughter found him and decided to rear him as her own. In adulthood, Moses witnessed the enslavement of his people, and killed an Egyptian in defense of a fellow Hebrew. The next day, when he sought to settle a dispute between two Hebrews, one retorted that he had no business in their affairs and asked if he intended to kill him as he had the Egyptian. Frightened that his murder was known, Moses ran off to the wilderness. There he found a wife and a job, tending a flock. He happened one day upon a flame in a bush that did not burn up, and thus encountered the God

of his ancestors, who had heard the cries of his people and had come
to deliver them through the leadership of a reluctant, inarticulate
Moses. When Moses finally agreed to approach Pharaoh, he was nat-
urally rebuffed, and Pharaoh got nasty and made the work of the Hebrews tougher, prompting them to turn on their new leader.

To make a long story short (see Exodus 1–15), ten plagues later
Pharaoh unwillingly let God's people go to celebrate a festival to
their God in the wilderness. But Pharaoh had a change of heart and
his armies gave chase, only to be destroyed in the Red Sea (Hebrew:
Sea of Reeds), which God parted for the Hebrews but sent crashing
down on the Egyptians—but not before the Hebrews, in their fear,
complained, "Was it because there were not graves in Egypt that
you have taken us away to die in the wilderness? What have you
done to us, bringing us out of Egypt? Is this not the very thing we
told you in Egypt, 'Let us alone and let us serve the Egyptians'? For
it would have been better for us to serve the Egyptians than to die
in the wilderness" (14:11–12). Thus began the great whine as they
wound their way through the wilderness for forty years, missing the
food and water and shelter that their oppression had afforded them.

But they were on their way to the promised land, and along the
way they stopped at God's holy mountain, where Yahweh had appeared to Moses in a burning bush: Mount Sinai, according to one
tradition; Mount Horeb, according to another. There they were
given the covenant of the law—represented by the Ten Commandments—that promised God's presence among them as long
as they followed God's law, a law intended to bring social harmony and personal integrity.

Our coming out as a community parallels the Hebrews coming
out of Egypt. Many of our scholars have recounted how much and
how often lesbians and gay men have contributed to history, culture,
and religion, as Joseph and his people contributed to the well-being
of the Egyptians. Yet the present "pharaohs" have forgotten, though
they are perfectly willing to accept our gifts anonymously from the
enslavement of the closet—whether of history or the present day. As
our strength as a community increases, the pharaohs of our time feel
it necessary to impose rules to keep us in line, banning our partici-

pation in the church, our rights in society, and our celebration of marriage. Scientific research, long focused on what causes "the problem" of homosexuality, may inadvertently create a way to discern and abort homosexually predisposed fetuses, just as Pharaoh decreed the death of Hebrew boy babies. Such an outlandish possibility is hardly necessary in a society that already so deeply attacks our sense of worth that gay teens are several times more likely to commit suicide than their straight counterparts and our youth and adults are too often driven to self-destructive lifestyles of drugs, alcohol, and unsafe sex. But despite the odds, like the Hebrews, the more we are oppressed, the stronger we become, throwing our oppressors into crisis.

Our leaders, like Moses, are imperfect, often raised up by circumstance or—to the eyes of faith—by providence to lead us out of the closet as a community. We have often rebuked them, demanding to know why we should follow. When their agitation has annoyed our pharaohs, who then take notice of us and clamp down on us all the harder, we may take it out on our own leaders, questioning their strategy, doubting their ability. When finally free of the closet, we may whine about what we have lost. In the wilderness, we sometimes forget about where we are going—a land promised for us, a place of equality, integrity, dignity, reconciliation, affirmation, and more light.

Our ten percent of the population may be experienced much like the ten plagues—a nuisance, an irritation, a threat to society and the family. I know that figure is disputed, but if we include bisexual and transgendered women and men, we are more than ten percent! However few or however many, we are clearly able to set our society and our church into a crisis that makes them want to be rid of us—sent off into the wilderness, excommunicated from the church. But, also like the pharaoh of Egypt, our pharaohs are ambivalent: at the same time that they are terrified of us, they want us back. They want us as members of their churches, singers in their choirs, donors to their causes, volunteers in their efforts, voters in their campaigns. But the operative word here is *their* rather than *our*.

Yet, just as the Israelites came out into the wilderness to celebrate a festival to God, find their holy mountain, and discover their law, so we too come out from the dominant culture and mainstream religion to celebrate our Pride festivals, discover our sacred sanctuaries (our Mount Sinais), and discern our organizing principles (our "commandments") as a community and as a congregation (in the broader sense of that term). With Miriam the prophet we dance on the shores of our deliverance; with Moses we glow from our encounter with God; and with the people of Israel we are empowered for the journey.

COMING OUT OF THE WILDERNESS

Numbers 13–14 tells the story of the Israelites' initial encounter with the promised land. In the Hebrew Bible, the book of Numbers is better named "In the Wilderness." When the Israelites first came within sight of the land God promised them, the land of Canaan, Moses sent spies to gather information for its conquest. Though they discovered the land flowing "with milk and honey," the majority of the military scouts thought the inhabitants unconquerable. "The land that we have gone through as spies is a land that devours its inhabitants," they said, "and all the people that we saw in it are of great size . . . and to ourselves we seemed like grasshoppers, and so we seemed to them" (Numbers 13:32–33). The people complained, "Would that we had died in the land of Egypt! Or would that we had died in this wilderness! . . . Let us choose a captain, and go back to Egypt" (14:2, 4b).

This lack of faith angered God, who sentenced them to forty more years in the wilderness, so that the unfaithful generation brought out of Egypt would die off, leaving their offspring to inherit the land promised them. Only Moses himself and the two spies, Caleb and Joshua, who brought a favorable report of the Israelites' ability to defeat the Canaanites, would be spared (though eventually even Moses got on the wrong side of God and was not allowed to cross over the River Jordan). Much of the Israelites' time in the wilderness was spent at an oasis named Kadesh-barnea.

Coming out of the wilderness proved in some ways as difficult as coming out of oppression. The majority report of the spies concluded that, even with God alongside, the Israelites were not the equal of the Canaanites. That oasis seemed so comfortable compared to the efforts required to claim the promised land! After God said their lack of faith disabled them from acquiring it at this time, some of them determined otherwise and "presumed to go up to the heights of the hill country, even though the ark of the covenant of the LORD, and Moses, had not left the camp. Then the Amalekites and the Canaanites who lived in that hill country came down and defeated them" (Numbers 14:44–45).

Many of us in the lesbian and gay community have found an oasis on our way to the promised land, and have decided to settle for less than full citizenship, either in the political realm or in the realm of God. Some of us feel we cannot possibly be the match of our opponents—or even of those who presently dominate the land God has *also and already* given us to inhabit. Many of our supporters and our own leaders tell us that "gradualism" is the way to accomplish our equality, mistaking this minimum goal of our struggle as a strategy. A few have launched into enemy territory without the rest of the community and have been defeated. Some have nostalgically whined for the good old days of the closet.

That we have not accomplished our goals in the short time we hoped discourages many of us and reinforces doubts of our capability of capturing our share of the promised land. But listening to naysayers or allowing ourselves to be placated by those who say "Be patient!" may not be God's will for our lives. I agree with David Mixner's assessment in his excellent book, *Stranger Among Friends,* that minorities do not achieve equal rights by sitting back and letting "progress" work its course.[2] Rights must be *expected, demanded, now.* Agitation and discomfort prompt change. But change cannot be achieved by skirmishes of small bands like Queer Nation or ACT Up, like the Israelites who presumed to settle the land without the rest of their people, the ark of the covenant, and their leader, Moses. Nor do I believe that the change we seek can

2. *David Mixner,* Stranger Among Friends *(New York: Bantam Doubleday Dell, 1996).*

be accomplished by violence, though this could be implied by my metaphorical use of the Israelite conquest of Canaan. Agitation and discomfort are more effective when they grow from others' experiences of solidarity with, compassion for, pleasure in, and love of us, whatever the nature of our relationship with them. More of our community must be involved in traditional channels of change, from organizing voting blocs and developing coalitions with other minorities to transforming conservative institutions, such as denominations, corporations, and political parties. Otherwise we will be condemned to living our lives in the wilderness or at an oasis (gay and lesbian urban ghettos/lesbian and gay congregations) or return to the slavery of Egypt, the closet. Especially those of us who are people of faith must reassure our community that victory is possible, that God is with us as one who always identifies with the victims of injustice. It is our responsibility to carry the ark of God's covenant with our people into the struggle for the promised land.

COMING OUT TO LOVE

Our opponents in the church frequently point out that no passages in the Bible affirm homosexuality. That may be true in the strictest sense, especially since the word never appears in the original languages in which scripture was written. But in our own self-affirmation, we who are lesbian, gay, and bisexual are making an affirmation that goes beyond sexual expression. We affirm God's gift and our right *to love*. No opposite-gender love story in scripture covers as many chapters as two same-gender love stories. First and Second Samuel devote many pages to the extraordinarily passionate relationship between David and Jonathan. An entire book of the Bible (albeit a short one) is devoted to the story of love and loyalty that Ruth demonstrates toward Naomi. It does not matter whether these covenant relationships included expressions of genital sexuality. What spiritually justifies any relationship, whether with God or with another, is love. Our opponents will quibble with such a statement, coming up with all kinds of supposed exceptions. But to criticize our loving, sexual relationships, they have to attack the *genuineness* of our love. Rather than do that, they have opposed *expressions* of our love as if they were rooted in anything but love. That was the mistake of the Pharisees, according to Jesus—judging someone by externals (Luke 11:37–41), by form rather than by content.

The first Israelite king, Saul, harshly judged his own son Jonathan for his expression of love. Though Israel had no established tradition of hereditary kingship, Jonathan would have had every right at least to fight for his father's throne at the end of Saul's reign. The Bible says that God, displeased with Saul, ordained otherwise, secretly choosing Jesse's youngest son, David, to end Saul's reign and take his throne. After David slew Goliath, Jonathan was smitten with love at first sight: "When David had finished speaking to Saul, the soul of Jonathan was bound to the soul of David, and Jonathan loved him as his own soul" (1 Samuel 18:1). Then Jonathan made a covenant with David by an unusual act of vulnerability: stripping off his own robe and armor and giving it to David to wear, offering him also his sword, his bow, and his belt. Even by today's standards of macho manhood, this would be considered a powerful testament of giving up control to another man, coming out of power because of love. No wonder Saul would later accuse Jonathan of choosing "the son of Jesse to your own shame" (1 Samuel 20:30).

Jonathan defended David against his father's wrath. When it became clear that David had to flee Saul's rage, David and Jonathan had a poignant farewell, a portrayal of intimacy never seen in the Bible between a man and a woman, and one never seen again until Jesus' own displays of intimacy with his disciples. "They kissed one another, and wept with one another, until David exceeded himself" (1 Samuel 20:41, RSV). I use here the footnoted possible translation of "exceeded" from the RSV, obscured by the more recent translation and footnote in the NSRV, which renders the "uncertain meaning" of the Hebrew as "David wept the more." In *Jonathan Loved David*, Tom Horner suggests that "exceeded" in the original Hebrew carries the ambiguous (possibly sexual?) connotation of the English word that renders it.[3] Earlier the men had exchanged vows, covenanting to protect one another and one another's house-

---

3. Tom Horner, Jonathan Loved David: Homosexuality in Biblical Times *(Philadelphia: Westminster Press, 1978).*

holds, a promise David would keep with Jonathan's disabled son, Mephibosheth (referred to in 1 Chronicles as Merib-baal). At the conclusion of that exchange, "Jonathan made David swear again by his love for him; for he loved him as he loved his own life" (20:17).

When both Saul and Jonathan were killed in battle, David lamented in an eloquent and elegiac psalm, "How the mighty have fallen! . . . Saul and Jonathan, beloved and lovely! . . . I am distressed for you, my brother Jonathan; greatly beloved were you to me; your love to me was wonderful, passing the love of women" (1 Samuel 1:19b, 23a, 26). Coming out of a position of power to love, Jonathan lost a throne but gained a heart, offering us the primary condition for all loving relationships: a willing vulnerability, a willingness to share power and control.

The book of Ruth tells us that a famine in the land caused Elimelech and Naomi and their two sons to flee their hometown of Bethlehem in their native Judah and live in the country of Moab, where their sons married Moabite women, whose people were at odds with the Israelites. Elimelech and the sons died, leaving Naomi and her daughters-in-law, Orpah and Ruth, to fend for themselves. This was an especially difficult circumstance for women of that day, for their status as women made them largely dependent on men economically. None of them had children, the ancient retirement plan, someone who would care for them in old age.

Naomi decided to return home to Bethlehem, where she had relatives who could help her survive. Her daughters-in-law intended to accompany her, but Naomi urged them to return to their homes. Orpah agreed reluctantly, but Ruth insisted upon going with Naomi, clinging loyally to her. Her cry of commitment was so powerful it is sometimes used in marriage ceremonies today:

> Do not press me to leave you
>   or turn back from following you!
> Where you go, I will go;
>   where you lodge, I will lodge;
> your people shall be my people,
>   and your God my God.
> Where you die, I will die —

there will I be buried.
May the LORD do thus and so to me,
and more as well,
if even death parts me from you!
(Ruth 1:16–17)

Upon their return to Naomi's hometown of Bethlehem, they gleaned fields together to survive. Then Naomi cleverly arranged a marriage for Ruth with Boaz, and Ruth soon presented Naomi with a son, a means of support for them both in old age. Naomi's women friends told her, "Blessed be the LORD, who has not left you this day without next-of-kin . . . for your daughter-in-law who loves you, who is more to you than seven sons, has borne him" (Ruth 4:14–15). Naomi herself nurses the child, who will link Ruth to the royal lineage leading to David and, much later, to Jesus.

This story is familiar to many of us. It has been viewed as a story of ancient feminism about two women who managed to survive the best way they could in the face of two famines: a famine of food, but more important, a famine of economic opportunity and independence for women. It has also been recognized as a story of same-gender love about Ruth, whose love for another woman occasioned her coming out of her home, her family, her country, and her religion to adopt the home, family, country, and faith of her beloved, Naomi.

Many women among us recognize in this story their own economic challenges in a society that still suffers from a famine of opportunities for women, a famine more severe for lesbians, bisexuals, transgendered women, women of color, single mothers, and women with disabilities. Some women have felt obliged to take the "Boaz option" and marry heterosexually for reasons other than love. This has served and still serves as a survival technique for many, especially among the poor and poorly educated.

Many women also hear in this story their own story of love for another woman, a commitment that calls them to come out from other loyalties—previous commitments of marriage and family, sometimes their communities, occasionally their religions, and often their former images of God. Within the story many women and men hear a call to come out to a different love, which may lead to a new "country," a new understanding of God, a new people, a new family, and a new home.

All of us who grow to accept and affirm our sexuality have in some sense heard this call to come out. In grief and regret, some of us may feel forced to leave a family, a congregation, or a community (much as Ruth did) to make our commitments. Following Ruth and Naomi's strategy, we use what is available to us in the church and society to survive. Yet, alongside Ruth and Naomi, we use our commitment to lovers, our fresh understandings of God, and our new communities of faith—maybe a support group, a network, an organization, a congregation—to thrive.

In these groups or in public gatherings or in private moments with family, friend, or lover, each of us might assure one another with this version of Ruth's vow that I wrote for the *Coming Out* liturgy (see chapter 7), a vow that echoes God's promise to be with us:

> We will never abandon you!
> Where you go, we will be there;
> what is life to you will be vital for us.
> Your people will be our own,
> and your God will be our God.

COMING OUT OF PRIVILEGE

For some, it is a puzzle why the book of Esther made it into the Bible, for God is never mentioned. Yet it is a book about both the essence and the result of spirituality, that is, a book about coming out of places of privilege to identify courageously with one's people and with the oppressed for the sake of justice.

Esther advanced in the court of King Ahasuerus without his knowing her Jewish identity. Indeed, she became queen. The evil prince Haman, angry that a Jew named Mordecai would not bow to him, urged the destruction of all Jews in the land. He told King Ahasuerus, "There is a certain people scattered and separated among the peoples in all the provinces of your kingdom; their laws are different from those of every other people, and they do not keep the king's laws, so that it is not appropriate for the king to tolerate them. If it pleases the king, let a decree be issued for their destruction, and I will pay ten thousand talents of silver into the hands of those who have charge of the king's business, so that they may put it into the king's treasuries" (Esther 3:8–9).

Mordecai learned of Haman's plan and challenged Esther, his cousin whom he had adopted, to intervene with the king. But Esther knew she risked her life in doing so, not only in confronting anti-Jewish sentiment head-on, but also because to approach the king without invitation meant death, unless the king raised his royal scepter in welcome.

When Mordecai received word of Esther's hesitation, he sent back this message: "Do not think that in the king's palace you will escape any more than all the other Jews. For if you keep silence at such a time as this, relief and deliverance will rise for the Jews from another quarter, but you and your [parents'] family will perish. Who knows? Perhaps you have come to royal dignity for just such a time as this" (Esther 4:13–14).

Esther asked Mordecai to have her people fast for her. She went in to the king, and he raised the golden scepter. Through careful and strategic planning, Esther was able to discredit Haman and thwart his plans to destroy her people. Their enemies were destroyed, and the Jews today celebrate Purim, a holiday "of feasting and gladness, days for sending gifts of food to one another and presents to the poor" (Esther 9:22).

Not long ago, a survey asked men what they most feared in their relations with women. They responded that they most feared being laughed at. When women were asked what they most feared in their relations with men, they said that they most feared being killed. And gay men wonder why lesbians feel more vulnerable than we do! As startling a revelation as this is for our day and age, think how much more that fear may have been for women of Esther's day.

Think about your own fear in first talking about your sexuality or gender identity with someone else, identifying yourself as lesbian, gay, bisexual, or transgendered. Imagine doing so within a government or a church or a corporation in which you have risen in the ranks to a place of honor and prestige. Then imagine doing

so in Nazi Germany, and you have a sense of Esther's predicament
and risk, as well as her courage, in coming out to save her people.

"There is a certain people scattered . . . among the peoples . . .
[whose] laws are different." Haman's words should sound familiar. Gay people are continually portrayed by those who oppose us
and many in the media as "choosing an alternative lifestyle" that
is perceived as lawless and loose rather than governed by the same
kinds of commitments and responsibilities that govern heterosexuals. Also, like the Jews of Esther's time, we are a minority "scattered" among the general population, which makes us vulnerable
and yet, contradictorily, frightening to others.

"If it pleases the king, let a decree be issued for their destruction, and I will pay ten thousand talents of silver into . . . the king's
treasuries," Haman offers. We might hear in this the religious right
approaching political candidates, bribing them either with pledges
of money or peril of opposition, depending on their stand on lesbian and gay rights. We might also hear anti-gay church members
manipulating the policies of congregations and denominations
with threats of lost revenues or the withholding of funds.

"Do not think that in the king's palace you will escape any more
than all the other Jews." Mordecai might as well be speaking to
gays and lesbians reluctant to intervene in the church and society
on behalf of their own people, those in closets reluctant to identify
with us, as well as those who have succeeded despite being out and
yet do nothing for the gay community. "For if you keep silence . . .
relief and deliverance will rise . . . from another quarter." Mordecai does not threaten to "out" Esther, for he knows the workings of
God's justice and resists the temptation to play God. Yet he also
knows the regret Esther will have if she does not play the privileged hand she has been dealt.

"Who knows? Perhaps you have come to royal dignity for just
such a time as this." Is this not only Mordecai's response to Esther,
but also God's response to our questions: Why did we have to be
born gay? Why do we have to endure prejudice? Why are the
church and the culture not more responsive to our concerns? Why
do we have to cope with AIDS?

Who knows whether we have not come to the church for such a time as this? Who knows whether we have not come to our nations and to our world for such a time as this? In reference to AIDS, who knows whether we have not come to the World Health Organization and the Centers for Disease Control and other health institutions for such a time as this? Belonging to our communities, local and global, entails struggling for what is right, whether in the realm of civil justice, religious justice, or medical justice.

Thus Esther asks that her people fast in solidarity with her. Fasting is a spiritual discipline: going *without* for a greater cause. It would have been accompanied by prayer, another spiritual discipline: going *within* for a greater cause. What Esther asks of her people is no less than our leaders should anticipate from us. We deserve no less from one another and from those who love us, for coming out itself is a spiritual discipline that involves going without and going within. We may give up much to be who we are and to be in solidarity with our people. We must go *within* to discover who we are and how we are called to serve our people.

Jewish solidarity gave Esther the courage to come out, transforming the climate for Jews in the Persia of her time, so that they might celebrate who they are in every time and place, especially during the festival of Purim. Our own solidarity in coming out will transform the climate for us in our time and place, so that we might celebrate our God-given love in every time and place, especially during our Pride festivals.

COMING OUT OF ANGER

Four brief chapters tell the story of Jonah, the world's most reluctant prophet, and yet the one who would receive the most immediate and total positive response. God called Jonah to preach repentance to the Ninevites, oppressors of his people, the Israelites. Instead, he boarded a boat bound for Tarshish, as far from Nineveh as possible. A storm arose, causing the sailors to call on their gods and to ask Jonah to call on his God for deliverance. Finally they cast lots to find who was responsible (a scapegoat) for their fate, and the lot fell on Jonah, whom they already knew to be "fleeing from the presence of the LORD" (Jonah 1:10). Reluctantly, they acceded to his suggestion to be thrown overboard, and a big fish swallowed Jonah, spewing him three days later back where he started. Jonah then went to Nineveh, and the Ninevites were immediately persuaded by his message, repenting and asking God's mercy, which God happily granted. "That's why I didn't want to go," Jonah basically complained to God. "For I knew that you are a gracious God and merciful, slow to anger, and abounding in steadfast love, and ready to relent from punishing" (4:2). Just as God challenged Cain's anger, God confronted Jonah's rage: "Is it right for you to be angry?" The message of this short book is that God is the God even of the Hebrews' oppressors, a theme of universalism found often in the prophetic books.

The same God in whose image we were created as lesbian and gay people, in whose grace and mercy we bask, by whose justice and love we are called, is the same God of the Nazi guard who tortured and murdered gay and lesbian Germans in concentration camps, the same God of the Vatican and the Christian Coalition and the mainstream denominations that actively persecute us today, the same God of the gay-basher who mutilates the bodies of lesbian sisters and gay brothers out of religious conviction. In our righteous anger, the lesson of Jonah is that we must not refuse or forget to offer our oppressors opportunities to turn from their shameful ways and discover the same God of grace and mercy, justice and love, that we enjoy. We must come out of our anger, so that those who oppress us do not, in a sense, victimize us twice by changing us into their likeness. We are made in the image of a gracious God, and we must serve as living reminders that they are too.

COMING OUT OF
"TRADITIONAL FAMILY VALUES"

His mother Mary was told that Jesus' own coming out would mean "that the inner thoughts of many will be revealed—and a sword shall pierce through your own soul too" (Luke 2:35). At twelve years of age, Jesus ignored his family's departure from Jerusalem to sit in the temple, his "Father's house" (2:49). He left his family and, as far as we know, never married and never "begat" children. He called his disciples away from their families (9:59–62), told them he had no home (9:57), and claimed that his gospel would "set a man against his father, and a daughter against her mother . . . and one's foes would be members of one's own household" (Matthew 10:35–36). When his family came to see him, he declared, "Whoever does the will of God is my brother and sister and mother" (Mark 3:35). Members of the new faith community would address one another as sisters and brothers. Jesus' family of choice included Lazarus, Martha, and Mary, three single siblings who lived together in Bethany.

Jesus was hardly concerned with traditional family values. In the New Testament, the biological, polygamous, prolifically procreative family of the Old Testament was superseded by the more vital, eternal, and extended family of faith, a family to be expanded by evangelism and inclusivity rather than mere procreation.

Jesus had a special word of defense for the eunuch, who was an outcast in Israel because his body was mutilated, but more important, because he could not procreate. In his teaching on marriage and divorce, Jesus exempted eunuchs who were born or made or self-chosen (which covers all possible ways we could be homosexual, doesn't it?—see Matthew 19:10–12). In clearing the area of the temple of Jerusalem where eunuchs (and other "strangers") could stand (Mark 11:15–18), Jesus quoted a text from Isaiah in which that prophet defended eunuchs:

> For thus says the LORD:
> To the eunuchs who keep my sabbaths,
>   who choose the things that please me
>   and hold fast my covenant,
> I will give, in my house and within my walls,
>   a monument and a name
>   better than sons and daughters;
> I will give them an everlasting name

> that shall not be cut off. . . .
> These I will bring to my holy mountain,
>   and make them joyful in my house of prayer;
> their burnt offerings and their sacrifices
>   will be accepted on my altar;
> for my house shall be called a house of prayer
>   for all peoples.
> Thus says the LORD God,
>   who gathers the outcasts of Israel,
> I will gather others to them
>   besides those already gathered.
>   (Isaiah 56:4–5, 7–8)

Notice *what* Jesus cleared for outcasts, including those who did not procreate—the ritual means of sacrifice: the tables of those who exchanged secular currency for temple coins with which the people could buy animals for sacrifice from other merchants. Being inclusive of outcasts was more important to Jesus than ritual and sacrifice. In the Acts of the Apostles (8:26–39), Philip would come across an Ethiopian eunuch (a double outcast) reading Isaiah, interpreted it, and baptized him on the spot.

First God, then Jesus, and then the church (through Philip) defended and welcomed the eunuch into the family of faith. Heterosexual procreation is not a requirement for membership. Long ago, the church came out of the closet of traditional family values.

COMING OUT AS OURSELVES

John's story of Jesus talking with the Samaritan woman at the well (John 4:1–42) serves as but one example of the way Jesus ignored barriers of religion, race, gender, and morality. Jesus disclosed himself as the Messiah to a person whose people practiced a religion at odds with his own, whose race was mixed and unacceptable to "purebred" Israelites, whose gender made her a subordinate, and whose multiple marriages and current unmarried living situation made her morally indefensible in those times even if not her fault. (Her husbands could have died or divorced her, for example, and her current situation may have reflected economic dependence.) Moreover, she was an outcast from her own people, judging from the fact that she came alone to draw water in the middle and in the heat of the day, when other women would have gathered water from the well in groups in the early morning. It was then that Jesus chose to speak with her, asking for a drink of water, in turn offering her "living" water that would quench her spiritual thirst. She returned to her own people and urged them to come meet Jesus, thus becoming the first evangelist. Her people told her, "It is no longer because of what you said that we believe, for we have heard for ourselves, and we know that this is truly the Savior of the world" (John 4:42).

Central to her transformation, however, was Jesus' penetrating knowledge of her: "You are right in saying, 'I have no husband'; for you have had five husbands, and the one you have now is not your husband. What you have said is true!" (John 4:17–18). Thus Jesus prompts the woman to say, "Sir, I see that you are a prophet" (4:19). She realizes his spiritual power by his ability to see her as she is. Even with such intimate knowledge, Jesus offers her living water.

Here the historical Jesus parts ways with the later church, the church would feel compelled to judge her and require confession before it would offer her any eternal mysteries. Jesus meets her in her closet and communes with her there with no preconditions, offering his own secret of being the Messiah, a title he resists in other contexts.

In the world and in the church, we feel compelled to keep up a persona of respectability in our quest for acceptance. When we are out of the closet, we may live in still another closet, cloaking ourselves with "acceptable" beliefs and behaviors, fearful lest our "true" nature be revealed. Yes, there are things about our nature we might wish to change. But transformation does not come by pretending that Jesus is not already inside our closets, communing with us, sharing his most intimate secret: that *God* loves us, that God *loves* us, that God loves *us*.

COMING OUT FOR GRACE

The zealous persecutor of Christians, the Pharisee Saul, could have as easily been a product of the Christian religion of our time as he was a product of the Jewish religion of his time. Though Jesus spoke of the Spirit of God as a wind that "blows where it chooses" (John 3:8), religion by definition can only serve as a windmill hoping to catch that wind and transform its power into a raison d'être for an institution—in other words, another closet. An institution or closet is by nature structured, rigid, confining, and limiting. It serves the purpose of having a "place" and keeping things altogether, but it obviously may block the course as well as be the channel for the winds of the Spirit.

The law was and is a "place," in a sense, for keeping things altogether, whether it be as profound as the law of Moses or as prosaic as the laws of religious fundamentalism. Saul enjoyed the security of the law, and the followers of Jesus were law-breakers, heretics, to him. We forget that Saul was a good and holy man, as had been those religious leaders who favored Jesus' death. But keeping religion sacred to Saul required sacrifice of those who defiled the practice of true religion, those Jewish sectarians who ultimately became known as Christians and moreover evangelized among Gentiles who did not first become practicing Jews.

Saul had his own transforming encounter with Christ (Acts 9:1–22; Galatians 1:13–17) and he became Paul, a central interpreter of God's grace in Jesus Christ, writing eloquently of it in many epistles that were among the earliest Christian writings and form much of the New Testament. Throughout Christian history, whenever our religion calcified, movements of the Spirit broke us out of our ossification, codification, and "theoclosetization" (yes, my own word). The maxim of "the Reformed church always reforming" is an affirmation of the church's need periodically to break out of comfortable closets of supposed orthodoxy. Saul-turned-Paul serves as a metaphor for the Spirit's coming out of any humanly made religion or institution or codification, no matter how inspired. Perhaps that is why, despite his own human limitations, Paul has captured the spiritual imagination of Christians throughout the centuries.

Coming out of the closet as a sexual minority also requires breaking free of confining expectations that previously governed and possibly inspired our lives. In busting open our closets, however, we discover that we have inhabited closets within closets. The outer closets we share with others whose sexuality and spirituality are confined by centuries-old accretions of expectations of how the two correlate. Together we must come out of a closet that relegates sexuality to the shadow side or the merely functional side of life (as procreative) to discover its sacred nature as both embodied experience and sensual expression of spirituality. Trusting God's limitless grace, we may then venture forth to life beyond both spiritual legalism and sexual fundamentalism.

COMING OUT EMPOWERED

My most vivid memory of my professor of New Testament, Luke Johnson, was his declaration in class that what separated Christianity from the pack of cults developing at the beginning of the common era was neither a superior theology nor ethics, but an incredible infusion of power—that of the Holy Spirit. That is what Christians celebrate on what is called the "birthday" of the church: Pentecost, when the Spirit that Jesus had promised the disciples descended upon a discouraged, disheartened, and possibly disillusioned gathering.

> And suddenly from heaven there came a sound like the rush of a violent wind, and it filled the entire house where they were sitting. Divided tongues, as of fire, appeared among them, and a tongue rested on each of them. All of them were filled with the Holy Spirit and began to speak in other languages, as the Spirit gave them ability. (Acts 2:2–4)

Not coincidentally, the Spirit arrived on the Jewish festival of Pentecost, celebrated fifty days (hence the name) after Passover to commemorate the gift at Mount Sinai of their covenant with God, which included the Mosaic law. Strangers "from every nation under heaven" (Acts 2:5) were in Jerusalem for the Jewish holy day, and were amazed "because each one heard [the disciples] speaking the native language of each" (2:6).

Jesus' disciples were "empowered" two millennia before our century made the word a cliché. But notice what they were empowered to do: to *communicate* the gospel; in a sense, to offer *communion* through words that made their good news accessible to everyone. The Spirit inspired their coming out of hiding to proclaim God's Word boldly. The contrast with the story of the tower of Babel is clear: God confused the language of those who would build a structure to gain access to God's heaven on their own terms, yet God empowers those who would build Christ's church with the ability to speak in the languages of strangers.

That, too, is our power in coming out. We are able to offer the good news of our identity and of our understanding that sexuality and spirituality may dance joyfully together. We may serve as one more reminder to the church that it consists of strangers, of outcasts, of those once and present victims of official power and authority with whom Jesus stood and stands. Because we are diverse in religion and race and condition, we may proclaim our gospel in every kind of language under heaven.

The Spirit has descended mightily on us. No matter how good our theology or how moral our ethics, it is the Holy Spirit manifest in our lives that will communicate the inspiration that we are also members of Christ's church, heirs with Christ, and citizens of God's commonwealth. Such communication is the essence of Communion as well as the essence of coming out. This power is not power *over* others, such as Jonathan gave up out of love for David; rather, it is the ability to tell our stories to the ends of the earth. Just as the apostle Peter witnessed the power of the Holy Spirit manifest in the lives of Gentiles in Acts 10 and 11, the church will witness the Spirit in us and confess with him, "I truly understand that God shows no partiality" (Acts 10:34).

CONCLUSION

By re-viewing biblical stories using the hermeneutical key of coming out, Bible characters live once more and reveal yet more light: greater spiritual insight than we may have previously imagined. This is a traditional process of biblical interpretation, though the familiar texts have been explored with a contemporary metaphor: coming out. The few examples of this chapter have revealed that coming out as ourselves and as dreamers, coming out for human love and for God's grace, means coming out of shame, oppression, wilderness, privilege, power, the familiar, our anger, traditional family values, the ghetto, legalism, and fearful silence. If we are to "test the spirits to see whether they are from God" (1 John 4:1) in regard to these conclusions, we must compare them with God's own coming out, to which we now return.

5

God Comes Out

AVOIDING STEREOTYPES
AND NAME CALLING

Hebrew tradition from ancient to modern times forbids any graphic representation of God. The second commandment bans such images and sets Judaism apart from the common practice of other ancient religions that, in a sense, tried to capture their god or gods in figures and pictures: "You shall not make for yourself an idol, whether in the form of anything that is in heaven above, or that is on the earth beneath, or that is in the water under the earth. You shall not bow down to them or worship them, for I the LORD your God am a jealous God" (Exodus 20:4–5). No wonder that the Christian notion of Jesus' divinity was viewed as heretical and reason for casting early Jewish Christians out of synagogues! A rigorous application of this commandment later caused the beheading of statues and the destruction or removal of great works of art in the cathedrals of Europe and England by some Protestants. Jesus was taken off the cross, and the venerated crucifix of Catholicism became the empty cross of the Reformers. The inherent wisdom in the iconoclasm of the Hebrews is illustrated by the twentieth-century theologian Karl Barth, who claimed a theologian's frustrating task of describing God was like that of an artist trying to depict a bird in flight—as soon as its image is committed to canvas, the bird is somewhere else.

When Moses sought God's name as he stood before the burning bush, he received the enigmatic answer, "I AM WHO I AM," which may better be translated "I will be what I will be" (Exodus 3:14). Either way, God is mysterious and elusive. This resistance of God to give up the sacred name (as was also true of Jacob's divine wrestler in Genesis 32:29–30) was based on an ancient belief that to have another's name gave one power. This helps explain why the third commandment comes so hard on the second, forbidding the misuse of God's name: "You shall not make wrongful use of the name of the LORD your God, for the LORD will not acquit anyone who misuses [God's] name" (Exodus 20:7). Unlike other ancient deities, this God was not about to be messed with, to be manipulated by magical incantations. Thus "Yahweh," the Hebrew name for the God of the Israelites, was never spoken aloud. In reading scripture to the people, the Hebrew term for "Lord" (*Adonai*) was substituted for "Yahweh." In the same vein of refusing to limit God, many Christians today substitute the gender-neutral word "Sovereign" for the male "Lord."

We can easily understand God's reluctance to her/his image being portrayed or name being used. As lesbian, gay, bisexual, and transgendered people, we often grit our teeth to see representations of us, whether on the news, in movies, television and radio programs, plays, books, and the visual arts. Knowing the stereotypes by which we are characterized and understanding how infrequently we are visible, we are more sensitive to portrayals of us that represent our community in an incomplete or unbalanced way. In this we are not unlike other minorities overcoming prejudice. Even realistic depictions of an eccentric or negative gay character are problematic until the media adequately portray the majority of us as positive and ordinary. Political correctness policing or censorship of either the media or our community (whose diversity delights me) is problematic and of doubtful effectiveness, so I appreciate the work of organizations like GLAAD (Gay and Lesbian Alliance Against Defamation) that offer responsible feedback to the media and challenge our community not to settle for false or misleading images of ourselves. We must be aware how the flamboyant or offensive gay or lesbian character plays into the hands of the dominant culture that likes to see us as abnormal and perverse creatures rather than as human beings like themselves. Better to throw the dominant culture into a Girardian mimetic crisis by demonstrating our sameness rather than fueling their feelings of superiority by parading before them outlandish actions, dress, and lifestyles. To loosely paraphrase Jesus, "Don't wear your pearls before swine!" (See Matthew 7:6.)

We may also comprehend God's hesitancy to give out her/his

name to someone who might not respect either the name or whom it represents. When we first came out, we too may have been resistant to giving out our names to people we met. Some of us used an alias, others offered only a first name, still others no name at all. When I first came out, my initial attempt to meet other gay men was to respond to three personal ads "seeking sincere friendship and possible relationship." I typed but did not sign my name, believing that if the recipient proved untrustworthy, I could claim an impostor wrote the letter. I, too, was resistant to giving power to another through my name.

Long before coming out, others seemed to have names for us: sissy, tomboy, fairy, pansy, dyke, faggot, queer, punk, homosexual. That is why claiming our name has been so important for us. Though the term "gay" has always seemed strange to me, I have worn it proudly rather than let our opposition name me. I like "lesbian" better because of its ancient historical roots in the poet Sappho and her female companions on the island of Lesbos, and it does not surprise me that many of my sisters choose this name rather than one derived from their brothers. I relish the in-your-face attitude of those who reclaim their positive identity by transforming "bad" words into good words: dyke, fairy, faggot, queer. There is something very strong and sexy and daring in doing so — and something very right and spiritual. After all, the term *Christian* was originally a derogatory designation. The obvious problem is that in certain contexts these words serve to reinforce the majority culture's view of us as too different to be "one of them" and therefore expendable.

Some among us rightly resist labels. This might originate in homophobia, a fear and self-hatred that virtually all of us will spend our lives unlearning as well as undoing its effects upon us. But it may also arise from reasons parallel to God's own avoidance of a single name or metaphor or image by which to be represented. Some of us simply do not want to be viewed as a gay actor, a lesbian teacher, a bisexual minister, or a transgendered custodian anymore than other minorities might want to be known as a disabled actor, an African American teacher, a woman minister, or a Jewish custodian. Our minority experience may inform our vocations, but it does not necessarily limit them or us. Largely gay and lesbian congregations have long wrestled with whether to term themselves "gay churches," and individual believers have mixed reactions to the designation "gay Christians."

The way in which God's relationship with the people of faith was labeled also changed with time and circumstance. "I will be what I will be" was also the "God of Abraham, Isaac, and Jacob" (Exodus 3:15). God was both the national deity of Israel and the universal God of all nations. God was the deliverer from Egypt, lawgiver at Mount Sinai, sustainer and guide in the wilderness, strength and redeemer in struggles and battles, wisdom and understanding in Israel's folly and ignorance. Through Jerusalem God nursed the people, dandling them on her knees, "as a *mother* comforts her child" (Isaiah 66:10–13), just as the God of justice is "merciful and gracious, slow to anger and abounding in steadfast love . . . as a *father* who has compassion for his children" (Psalm 103:8, 13). We can understand the varied descriptions of God's relationship with God's people because the ways we designate our own relationships vary with time and place. Given the circumstance, we might describe our beloved as husband, wife, spouse, lover, friend, partner, lifemate, significant other, main squeeze, or better half. We use different metaphors to illustrate various characteristics of our beloved: my honey, my rock, my baby, my defender, my hero, my princess, my prince, my inspiration, my love, and so on. Similarly, the people of the Bible used different metaphors for God. It is because people of faith sometimes get stuck in their metaphors (to paraphrase Joseph Campbell)—confusing their metaphors with reality—that the God of the Bible resisted the making of graven images and the overuse and misuse of the divine name or of any single metaphor.

"PERSONING" THE ISSUE

As if the people were still not getting it right, misunderstanding both the nature of God and God's relationship with us, Christian scriptures affirm the Incarnation, that God became one of us to re-

veal more fully the divine nature. Many of the early church teachers believed that the Incarnation alone was redemptive. It is easy
to see how a Jew like Saul, orthodox in his faith, would take of-
fense at the notion that God could somehow be reduced to a mere
human body. If I were born and reared in Judaism, I too would
rightly have reservations about this incredible and sacrilegious
theological concept.

As the Gospel writer John theologized about it almost a century
after the birth of Jesus, the Logos (the Word) of God became flesh
and lived among us. The Logos is more than mere word. God's
Word called creation into being; for example, "God said, 'Let
there be light'; and there was light" (Genesis 1:3). "Now the word
of the LORD came to Jonah . . ." (Jonah 1:1) as it did to many of
God's servants, and we remember from chapter 4 that no matter
how Jonah tried to escape this word, the prophecy of Isaiah was
fulfilled once more:

> For as the rain and the snow come down from heaven,
>   and do not return there until they have watered the earth,
> making it bring forth and sprout,
>   giving seed to the sower and bread to the eater,
> so shall my word be that goes out from my mouth;
>   it shall not return to me empty,
> but it shall accomplish that which I purpose,
>   and succeed in the thing for which I sent it.
>
> (Isaiah 55:10–11)

God's Word is God's action in history. It was manifest time and
again in the story of the Israelites in Jewish scriptures. Though
there are exceptions (see pages 39–40), the Bible generally does
not depict God's Word as a weapon of violence but as an instrument of redemption, having the power to separate creation from
chaos, save earthly life from extinction in the flood, deliver the oppressed from oppressors, bring social harmony and justice out of
human anarchy and evil, and redeem humanity out of the wilderness of alienation from Creator and creation.

Inasmuch as God's Logos signifies both word and action, it was *logical,* then, to preserve God's action in history in both myth and ritual, in both scripture and sacrament as described in chapter 1. That is why worship consists of word and sacrament. Sacraments act out the myths of God's Word in history. Coming out as sacrament means recognizing God's Word acting in our own life, delivering us from the closet, guiding and sustaining us, and promising us a new and more meaningful life.

Christians would come to perceive God's Logos manifest in Jesus of Nazareth, a humble but passionate itinerant preacher from rural Galilee. Of course, that was probably their view in retrospect; thus the Gospel of John, written much later than the Epistles and the other Gospels, gives the grandest account of the eternal origin and ultimate meaning of Jesus the Christ. In Jesus' own day, his nature, his essence, was not grasped in the way it would eventually be understood. Indeed, this has been true throughout history regarding many people whose influence is not discerned until after they are gone. Some Gospel stories imply that the people "got it" then, but again, that is because the stories were written later with the benefit of hindsight. As in chapter 4, I am not going to get bogged down in biblical scholarship, not because I don't believe it to be good, right, and useful, but because the truths I wish to highlight are central to the myth of Jesus, the deeper spiritual significance of who he is, what he was about, and how he serves as God's Word for us. To try to get behind or underneath or on top of that myth may miss the point. Myth is another way for God to remain mysterious and elusive, and yet reveal dimensions of self that give us, with Moses, a kind of glimpse of God's backsides (Exodus 33:23). We may summarize that glimpse, the New Testament, from the perspective of coming out.

In the birth of Jesus, God comes out to us through union with human flesh—that of a woman, marginalized by her gender, her youth, her poverty, her unmarried yet pregnant state. God comes out to us as a baby born in the tiniest corner of the world, far from any place of power: in a stable in a strange town and in a land and culture dominated by a foreign power, the Roman Empire. Yet even in this vulnerable condition, this God-child attracted foreign mystics, temple prophets, local shepherds, and the wrath of a king who sought to destroy him. God comes out to us as an infant refugee in Egypt until the death of that king meant safety to return. God comes out to us as an adolescent son of a carpenter from the ghetto[1] of Nazareth, who once, around puberty, made a pilgrimage to the temple at Jerusalem where his insight amazed the teachers of the law. God comes out to us as a person who stepped from the crowd to be baptized by John the Baptist, followed by a confirmation of divine relatedness and belovedness. God comes out to us as a newly baptized wanderer in the wilderness baited by the Tempter, perhaps the same one who enticed Cain's violence and maybe Azazel, the demon of the desert that glutted itself on scapegoats. God comes out to us as one who refused the three temptations common to all: that of mere survival, turning stones to bread; that of credibility and certainty, proving divine right by jumping from the pinnacle of the temple; and that of absolute control, taking charge of the kingdoms of this world. To succumb to any of these temptations was to pay homage to the demon of the desert and the prince of this world that found the blood and carcasses of sacrificial scapegoats delicious.

In the ministry of Jesus, God comes out to us as a teacher, healer, comforter, challenger, and harbinger of the divine kingdom or commonwealth in which the downcast are uplifted and by which the year of divine favor is proclaimed. God comes out to us as a friend willing to die for friends, as a good shepherd willing to search for the lost lamb and lay down one's life to defend sheep, as one who calls us family based on faith rather than on blood, as one who washes the disciples' feet and offers them his own body and blood in a final meal. God comes out to us as one who hangs out with outcasts, the disreputable, the unorthodox, the marginalized, the ritually unclean. God comes out to us as one who defends women and eunuchs and those of mixed race (Samaritans) and responds to other races (the Roman centurion, the Syrophoenician woman). God comes out to us as one who weeps for opponents in Jerusalem, wishing to gather them as a mother hen gathers her brood.

---

1. *"Can anything good come out of Nazareth?" (John 1:46) implies a bad reputation.*

As the prophet Jesus, God comes out to us as one who dispar-
ages the self-righteous, the established, the powerful, the authorities, and the unloving application and the unjust avoidance of the
law. God comes out to us as one who commands obedience to the
intent and heart of the law: loving God, neighbor, and self. God
comes out to us as one who makes a home and establishes solidarity with political, economic, and ritual victims. God comes out
to us as temple custodian, removing the ritual clutter of temple
coins and animal sacrifices, reminding all who are attentive that it
should be "a house of prayer for all peoples," reopening the space
of the temple set aside for women, for alien converts, for eunuchs.
God comes out to us as one who, in life and in death, redeems us
from the power of sin and death and law, effecting atonement between God and human beings. God comes out as one who, from
the cross, offers mercy for those "who know not what they do,"
creates family between the beloved disciple and Jesus' mother, extends an inclusive paradise to a crucified criminal, and whose
Spirit rips open the veil separating the temple's holy of holies from
ordinary women and men while escaping from the cross.

As the resurrected Jesus, God comes out to us from our own
tombs of despair and grief, loss and death, and encourages us with
Mary, "Do not be afraid." God comes out as one who lives despite
human violence, a true survivor of human abuse and victimization,
whose Word and will for life and love does not return empty to the
divine and eternal and all-loving embrace, but restores us to Godself forever.

God comes out to us as Holy Spirit, as Comforter and Advocate,
as inspiring and empowering force. God comes out to us as flames
of passion that translate God's Word into the words of strangers at
Pentecost, proclaiming an evangelical, inclusive church—the
Body of Christ that is no longer simply a first-century Palestinian
Jewish man named Jesus, but now is Gentile and Jew, slave and
free, female and male, eunuch and procreator, all who suffer and
rejoice as one. God comes out to us as a gracious God, who desires
mercy rather than sacrifice, who establishes a new covenant of
grace by which we live, who writes the law of love not in stone but

on our hearts (Jeremiah 31:33; Hebrews 8:10). God comes out to us as God-with-us, as God-is-one-of-us, as God who will make a home with us, who will call us God's people, who will wipe every tear from our eyes, remove death's grasp and all mourning and crying and pain, and give birth to a new heaven and a new earth. As the visionary John ended Revelation, and thus the Bible: "Maranatha! Our Lord, come! The grace of the Lord Jesus be with all the saints. Amen" (Revelation 22:20).

The story of the New Testament is that God comes out of the closet of heaven and out of the religious system of the time to reveal Godself in the person of Jesus the Christ, whose Holy Spirit makes a home with us in a spiritual community identified as *ekklesia,* the called-out ones, the church, the Body of Christ. Indeed, Jesus and the Spirit reveal to Christians what really had been known in Judaism all along, that God is this-worldly, that God tabernacles with us, is gracious to us, cares for us, redeems us to Godself, and calls us as a witness of God's love for all peoples.

In Christian belief, Jesus provided an incarnation, an embodiment of the abstract notion of "God" and of the controversial issue of "God's agenda." We know, from our own experience, about providing an embodiment of the abstract notion of "homosexuality" and of the controversial issue of "the gay agenda." An encounter with God's Word-made-flesh converts an individual's opinion and experience of God. We know how personal encounters convert others' opinions and experience of gay, lesbian, bisexual, and transgendered people. Through our own experience of coming out we may comprehend God's process of coming out, what is formally referred to in theological circles as "revelation." The whole Bible is the story of God's coming out to us. The biblical writers saw God revealed in: the creation of the cosmos; the rainbow promise after the flood; a burning bush in the Egyptian wilderness; thunder and lightning on Mount Sinai; a still, small voice to Elijah on Mount Horeb; a stranger in a fiery furnace with Shadrach, Meshach, and Abednego; a defender of the marginalized; a Deity for all nations; a conception of Mary; and a compassionate rabbi and healer named Jesus.

Revelation as
Sacrificial Offering

A traditional Christian sacrament is viewed as instituted or ordained by God in the life of Jesus Christ. God comes out to us in the sacrificial offering of the life, ministry, teachings, death, and resurrection of Jesus Christ. Thus we may say that, in Jesus Christ, coming out—self-revelation, self-offering—is a sacred and holy act: a sacrament. In previous chapters, we have already noted how coming out bears the marks of a sacrament as it reveals the sacred in our midst, is both communal and creates community, serves as a means of grace, revitalizes participants, renews relationships, requires a believer's participation, and is observed in various forms throughout scripture. Coming out is biblical and Christian and sacramental. Coming out, then, is surely something to be celebrated, is it not?

We know from personal experience that coming out meets with hostility, prejudice, bigotry, ignorance, fear, hatred, prohibition, and violence. That is why coming out is a sacrificial offering: a sacrifice because of the risks we take, yet also an offering because of the gifts (charisms) that we bestow. The story of Jesus tells us we are not alone in this, that we have a friend in high places who knows exactly how we feel. God's own coming out in Jesus met with hostility, prejudice, bigotry, ignorance, fear, hatred, prohibition, and violence. Gay-bashing and God-bashing come from the same sources. Gay-bashers, of both street and pulpit variety, cite religious beliefs to justify their behavior just as God-bashers justified eliminating Jesus for religious reasons.

Jesus served as a sacrificial offering: a sacrifice because of the risk he took in unveiling God, yet also an offering because of the gifts of grace and of the Spirit that he bestows in doing so. Sacrificial offering does not *necessarily* mean violence, victims, martyrdom, and death. The sacred reveals itself not in violence but in vulnerability. God's presence is welcomed not by sacrifice but by openheartedness. In the words of Pope John Paul II, God exercises "a preferential option for the poor." In Luke's Sermon on the Plain, Jesus said, "Blessed are you who are *poor,* for yours is the kingdom of God" (Luke 6:20). In Matthew's Sermon on the Mount, this becomes, "Blessed are the poor *in spirit,* for theirs is the kingdom of heaven" (Matthew 5:3). The testimony of Jesus' life is that God is drawn to those marginalized by political, economic, and religious systems and structures.

For centuries, the marginalized, the oppressed, and the suffering looked to Jesus on the cross as giving meaning to their pain. Yet we may wish to rethink this approach in our own distress. Some Jews today refuse to apply the term *holocaust* to what they believe to be the meaningless suffering of those who died in Nazi concentration camps because the term has religious connotations, implying that their collective death was a sacred burnt offering to God, thus somehow redemptive and God-ordained. Instead they use the Hebrew word *shoah,* which simply means "annihilation," because there is no way that Nazis could be perceived as "priests" and no way to imagine the murders they performed as a "service" to God.

Those who are oppressed and view their suffering as somehow ordained by God are attributing priestly powers to tyrants and oppressors, no matter how whitewashed they may be by our society (for example: Congress, clergy, churches, etc.; see Matthew 23:27–28. Remember, it was the *good* people who crucified Jesus, not criminals or others judged as sinners). Worse, they are conceiving a God who implicitly desires violence, because suffering is the other side of violence. God is with us in suffering, but not because God wills violence. Violence has no sacred, God-ordained meaning, as Job found out, as the prophets pointed out, and as Jesus himself recognized in the experience of the cross: "My God, my God, why have you forsaken me?" (Matthew 27:46).

Earlier I wrote that I believed God was present at sacrifices trying to bring the severed parts of the animal together, trying to heal the breach, the wound, the separation, and trying to restore life. In the same way, I believe that God was surely present at the crucifixion, not as one who ordained this violence for the Beloved, but rather as one who wanted to save Jesus from his suffering and restore life to a crucified Christ. At the same time, the myth of Jesus as divine is that, in him, *God* is crucified for the atoning act of coming out (the Incarnation).

Jesus' sense of forsakenness on the cross reflects not the absence of God but the absence of sacred purpose in the violence being done to him, the absolute meaninglessness of excruciating pain—a pain unto death. How can we possibly believe it means anything else? Jesus' religious tradition acknowledged God's presence in every time and place; and the evolving theme of his tradition, of which he and his ministry serve as climax, is that God is especially with victims. Simply the fact that Jesus cried out to God from the cross suggests that Jesus believed that God was there, listening. Jesus quoted the beginning of Psalm 22, which ultimately expresses trust in God's faithfulness. Later, Jesus proclaimed from the cross, "Father, into your hands I commend my Spirit" (Luke 23:46).

THE FOLLY OF THE CROSS

If atonement is brought about by the Incarnation (God's coming out) and the violence of the cross is not redemptive, then what role does the crucifixion play?

Paul recognized that the cross was "a stumbling block to Jews and foolishness to Gentiles, but to those who are the called [-out ones], both Jews and Greeks, Christ the power of God and the wisdom of God. For God's foolishness is wiser than human wisdom, and God's weakness is stronger than human strength" (1 Corinthians 1:23–25). The folly of the cross leads directly into Paul's concept of the call:

Consider your own call, brothers and sisters: not many of you were wise by human standards, not many were powerful, not many were of noble birth. But God chose what is foolish in the world to shame the wise; God chose what is weak in the world to shame the strong; God chose what is low and despised in the world, things that are not, to reduce to nothing things that are, so that no one might boast in the presence of God. [God] is the source of your life in Christ Jesus, who became for us wisdom from God, and righteousness and sanctification and redemption, in order that, as it is written, "Let the one who boasts, boast in the Lord." (1 Corinthians 1:26–31)

The folly of the cross is as enigmatic as "I will be what I will be"!

Despite the appeal to folly, Paul here presents a carefully reasoned argument. "Nothing which is true or beautiful or good makes complete sense in any immediate context of history," wrote Reinhold Niebuhr, "therefore we must be saved by faith."[2] Essentially, this is what Paul means by "the foolishness of Christ crucified." It did not make sense in the Jewish or Greek or Roman context of his time. Since "the world did not know God through wisdom, God decided, through the foolishness of our proclamation, to save those who believe," Paul declares (1 Corinthians 1:21). Faith tells Paul and "those who believe" that God was somehow present in this foolishness and weakness—in Jesus' vulnerability to both Greeks and Jews (and by inference, to the Romans, since crucifixion was a Roman execution), who demand sound wisdom and signs of power. Moreover, the called-out ones (*ekklesia,* the church) are those who are not powerful, nobly born, wise, strong, elevated or beloved by the world—rather, they are those who are most vulnerable. Through Christ's identification (or solidarity) with them, God imparts righteousness and sanctification and redemption to them—the marks of holiness.

I believe that trying to make sense of the crucifixion to the Jews and the Romans and the Greeks (and all the other cultures in which sacrifice was practiced as part of both legal and religious systems) led Christianity onto a sacrificial path that has detoured us from God and the very gospel that Jesus proclaimed. Jews understood the sacrificial system of the temple, Romans understood the legal system of their empire, and Greeks understood philosophical logic, so the cross came to be understood in sacrificial, legal, and logical terms. From Paul to Anselm, from Luther and Calvin to Karl Barth, the "folly" of the cross was nonetheless rationally explained variously as expiation, propitiation, substitution, satisfaction, redemption, and compensation.[3] Would that we had re-

---

2. Reinhold Niebuhr, The Irony of American History *(New York: Charles Scribner's Sons, 1952), 63.*

3. *Lest I appear to dismiss such an eminent group of theologians and a dominant Christian understanding in one brief sentence, I must explain that better scholars than I can do justice to the history of our faith in relation to this issue. My purpose here is to open an avenue of thought for those who do not believe or are reluctant to believe that God in any way demanded the death of Jesus, and to connect that with the primary thesis of this book.*

mained "fools for the sake of Christ"! The church has buried Christ once more under sacrificial layers, the church has closeted Christ in a tabernacle on a sacrificial altar as a host waiting to be broken time and again. In Eastern Orthodox traditions, even this sacrifice is done behind a screen. Christians have veiled God once more, restored the curtain between us and the holy of holies, chosen safety in distancing ourselves from the sacred revelation of God by hiding behind a new sacrificial and priestly system.[4]

How we know that experience in our own coming out! Our culture has tried to explain homosexuality and bisexuality biologically, psychologically, theologically, morally, and socially, usually with the intent to keep us at a distance, to fix us, to prevent or avoid sexual difference, to categorize us, to regulate us, to criminalize us, to condemn us, to separate us from one another and from the heterosexual mainstream. With a similar distancing effect, our family and our friends often "politely" avoid or ignore the ramifications of our self-revelation, failing to inquire about or include our partners, faulting our need to be ourselves in all circumstances, discounting the depths of our feelings when sorrowing over the lack or the loss of a partner. We are often buried in our family's, society's, or the church's closet, only to be scapegoated and sacrificed every time our sexual identity comes out, is brought out, or is outed.

Years ago, the presbytery in which I resided voted on a motion to amend our denomination's constitution to include the sentence, "Governing bodies may ordain church officers without regard to sexual orientation." The vote was a tie, one that to some of us revealed God's wry humor: 69 to 69. The moderator of the presbytery could have either let the vote stand or cast a deciding vote. We thought he was with us, but he hemmed and hawed, and finally cast his vote against the amendment because, as he explained from

---

4. *In using metaphorical hyperbole to some extent here, I obscure the understanding of* mystery *in the sacrament. The early church used the Greek word* mysterion *to name the concept of the external reality of God's love. The Western church translated this word as* sacrament, *or sign. But the former term captures better the notion of having a peek at the Divine Mystery that, though it comes out in revelation, still remains partly hidden. We can understand how this may be so for, though we come out, part of us remains hidden in shadow and mystery, hidden by the very identity that reveals so much of who we are.*

the podium, of "three little letters" in the heart of the proposal: "S-E-X!" The incident revealed once more that those of us who come out as bisexual and lesbian and gay reveal a glory larger than our self-identity: we reveal the glory of sexuality itself, a divinely created and graciously given glory that the church has also veiled, demanding we veil our faces because we have seen in our sexuality the glory of God. We can get a finite inkling of the infinite frustration of God, who wants to share with us divine glory, yet is told by the church to keep veiled behind sacrificial stereotypes.

Ultimately, what is vital (in the sense of life-giving) and more readily discernible is not what effect the crucifixion has on God, but what effect it has on us. Even the goat sacrificed on the altar of Yahweh on the Day of Atonement was believed to purify the people rather than placate God, permitting a sinful people to continue to enjoy the presence of a holy God. The twelfth-century Christian theologian Peter Abelard taught that the crucifixion of Jesus calls out the compassion of human souls from the world's many distractions, enabling solidarity with all who suffer—victims. Compassion sets humans apart (one definition of "holy") from other creatures and makes us one with God because, I believe, compassion is the *imago Dei*, the image of God in which we were created.[5] Thus compassion of God and of human beings is one. Jesus prayed for his present and future followers "that they may be one, as we are one" (John 17:11), importuning, "As you, [God], are in me and I am in you, may they also be in us, so that the world may believe that you have sent me. The glory that you have given me I have given them, so that they may be one, as we are one, I in them and you in me, that they may become completely one, so that the world may know that you have sent me and have loved them even as you have loved me" (John 17:21–23).

---

5. I want to qualify my endorsement of Abelard's view that compassion sets us apart from other creatures. I believe that our ability to feel solidarity with Jesus on the cross is a unique human experience. But I have witnessed other creatures demonstrate compassion. For instance, my dog, Calvin, licks my face if I cry at a sad movie or if I am sick. Many stories exist of dolphins coming to the rescue of humans in trouble at sea. Chimpanzees show a range of emotions, including compassion. This mere sampling should serve to deflate our narcissistic human egos a bit.

Jesus awakens our compassion—that which unites us with God—
not in the violence of the cross but in his vulnerability on the cross,
the cross being the human response to Jesus coming out of heaven,

> who, though he was in the form of God,
>   did not regard equality with God
> as something to be exploited,
> but emptied himself,
>   taking the form of a slave,
>   being born in human likeness.
> And being found in human form,
>   he humbled himself and became obedient to the
>   point of death—
> even death on a cross.

(Philippians 2:6–8)

Jesus was executed because of those three little letters at the heart
of his gospel: "G-O-D." He was executed because he was accused
of revealing his divinity (Luke 22:66–71) and of wanting to destroy the temple (and thus its sacrificial system that closeted God;
Matthew 26:61).

Abelard thought of Jesus as a model of absorbing violence.
René Girard, whose theories of mimetic rivalry, scapegoating, and
sacrifice I have already described, was led by his own academic inquiry to become a Christian because he came to a similar insight:
that God has undone the sacrificial mechanism based on the notion
that violence and scapegoats are divinely required by becoming, in
Jesus, the innocent victim subjected to violence and scapegoating
who in turn refuses either to serve ultimately as a scapegoat (turning the crucifixion to resurrection) or to do violence and scapegoat
others ("Forgive them; for they know not what they are doing").
In so doing God unveils the scapegoat mechanism as spiritually
bankrupt. The violence of the crucifixion is a "human thing";
God's thing is life restored.

LIVING SACRIFICES

In the temple of the sacrificial system, Jesus was "the stone that
the builders rejected" even in the church that eventually and igno-

rantly resuscitated the sacred violence that God and the gospel message rejected. In relation to lesbian, gay, bisexual, and transgendered Christians today, church leaders still echo the high priest Caiaphas when he spoke to the Sanhedrin of Jesus' necessary death after Jesus resurrected Lazarus: "It is better for you to have one man die for the people than to have the whole nation destroyed" (John 11:50). The religious authorities plotted Lazarus's death as well (12:10–11). Jesus called Lazarus out as Jesus calls us out, and now some religious leaders plot not only our death by excommunication, but also the death of the inclusive, loving Body of Christ by stirring controversy, withholding funds, and threatening schism. Yet the Spirit of Christ refuses to rest in peace until the scapegoat mechanism that sacrifices victims is understood as the antichrist that it is. That is why Jesus promised us the Holy Spirit as Paraclete, that is, advocate or defender of innocent victims.

In a chapter of *The Scapegoat,* "The Demons of Gerasa," René Girard applies his theories to the story of the Gerasene demoniac (Luke 8:26–39). In the story, Jesus and his disciples came upon a naked man possessed by demons whose collective name is "Legion." He lived among the tombs outside the city in the country of the Gerasenes. Though temporarily restrained by the citizens of the city, the demoniac kept escaping, in Mark's version, to howl and bruise himself with stones night and day (Mark 5:5). Recognizing Jesus' power, the demons begged him to send them into a nearby herd of pigs rather than return them "into the abyss." Jesus did so, and the pigs rushed down a steep hill to be drowned in the sea. The Gerasenes heard what had happened and came to see Jesus. When they saw the demoniac clothed and in his right mind, they were afraid, and ultimately asked Jesus to leave! The former demoniac begged to go along, but Jesus insisted that he return home to proclaim among the Gerasenes what God had done for him.

Despite their possible annoyance at the loss of a herd of pigs, until Girard's explanation I always found the ending curious—the Gerasenes were afraid and asked Jesus to leave. The Gerasene demoniac served as a cyclical scapegoat, according to Girard; he carried within him the demons of the people of the city. When he escaped from his inadequate restraints and, in a sense, "stoned" *himself* among the dead, the city could live in peace. Jesus delivered the man from being the Gerasenes' scapegoat; and their demons died down a ravine, much like the Mishnah's description of the demise of the scapegoat (see page 29). In this instance, the scapegoat (the demoniac) was saved and the crowd (albeit, of demons) was sacrificed. Yet it is important to note that Jesus did not actually scapegoat even the demons; he merely put them in a herd of swine as they requested.

As I describe this, I notice parallels to the story, discussed in chapter 4, of the Samaritan woman at the well, but with opposite results. The Samaritans were converted by their scapegoat, while the Gerasenes were threatened by theirs.

I see parallels between our own story and that of the Gerasene demoniac. The demons of the majority culture and the church are laid upon us: the breakup of families; distress over loss of gender differentiation; disdain for sexuality; resistance to an embodied and sensual spirituality; their own faithlessness, idolatry, and narcissism; fear of their own same-gender attractions; anxiety about their own sexual inadequacies, sexual sins, sexual performance and dysfunction; sexual exploitation; adultery; rape; divorce; abortion; spousal and child abuse and molestation.

There is a parallel found in any culture and religion dominated by heterosexual males who blame their sexual feelings on women, from the subtlety of legislation prohibiting women rather than men from going shirtless to the outrageous justification of rape because a woman "asked for it." This male scapegoating of women is evident in many biblical stories, the most familiar being the story of the woman taken in adultery (John 7:53–8:11). The men are ready to stone her, but the reader might wonder, what about the man with whom she was caught? What did Jesus write on the ground that prompted them not to cast the first stone? Was their own desire for the woman made plain before them, or their own adulterous affairs, or the gender inequity of their administration of "justice"? Wasn't the scapegoat mechanism stripped of its religious justification by Jesus' defense, "Let anyone among you who is without sin be the first to throw a stone at her" (John 8:7)?

Like the Gerasene demoniac, as we are forced out or run away as the scapegoats of church and society, we carry either a little or a lot of these demons into our sense of selves as individuals and as a community. We may figuratively howl among tombstones and gash ourselves with rocks. Coming out begins the process of delivering us from whatever demons of self-hatred or self-doubt we may have. But coming out also means coming in, coming back into our selves and our church and our society, like the man Jesus sent back to the Gerasenes to "declare how much God has done for you." That man's return undoubtedly sent the Gerasenes into a crisis, just as we send our culture and our churches into a crisis by refusing to serve as their scapegoats.

Thus we serve as "the living sacrifice" referred to by Paul in Romans 12. If only our opponents spent as much time meditating on this chapter as they have wasted on Romans 1, falling for Paul's rhetorical argument about the absurd notion that God could ever give anybody up ("God gave them up . . . ," Romans 1:24)! We are called as living sacrifices—an oxymoron that redefines the nature of sacrifice—"transformed" as we "discern what is the will of God—what is good and acceptable and perfect," while not "conformed to this world" (12:2), especially its heterosexism. We are finally advised to avoid becoming like those who wish to scapegoat us: "Do not be overcome by evil, but overcome evil with good" (12:21).

When I still lived in West Hollywood, I would sometimes take personal retreats at Mount Calvary Retreat House in Santa Barbara, run by the Episcopal Order of the Holy Cross. During a prolonged stay, George Lynch came to visit me. The brothers all knew George, and, as they greeted him, one asked playfully, "What did you bring us?" George smiled broadly, opened wide his arms, and replied, "I brought myself!" The priest who had asked the question was amazed by his answer. He explained that he had served at the order's house in Africa, and when locals came to visit, they would bring no gifts, but they too would announce, "We bring ourselves!"

We bring ourselves, our greatest gift, living sacrifices, to a church and a society that are still learning that God desires mercy, not sacrifice.

6

Coming Out as Celebration

Those who are designated "saints" serve as living sacraments, revealing the holy in their lives and in ours as well. As sacraments manifest different aspects of the sacred, so do saints. I began this book with Ross Greek's philosophical perspective: "All of life is a sacrament!" Although Ross lived by this principle in his service to others, especially outsiders, his simple Quaker upbringing and his staid Presbyterian identity made him rather a Puritan in terms of personal and aesthetic pleasures. His constant battle for justice in the church and in society left him little energy or time merely to enjoy the sacred nature of life. He took pride in complaining about the rigors of his work, frequently pointing out that he had not taken a vacation in years. When I finally persuaded him to take one, he spent the time repairing and painting his house, because he feared his crippling back pain would eventually land him in a wheelchair. I worried that butting my head against the church as Ross had done most of his professional life would affect me the same way. Ross was truly a "living sacrifice," and he let you know it (as did Paul, who coined the phrase—see 2 Corinthians 11:23–29). I do not believe I am being patronizing to say that, though I loved him dearly, I also felt genuine pity for him.

In my first book, *Uncommon Calling,* I described a severe bout with mononucleosis in college that, mixed with feelings of abandonment just after I came out, led me to self-pity. On Christmas Day that year, I slept all but two hours. In my fevered state, the message of the Incarnation came to me, and I wrote this:

> Love is being crucified
> And rising again
> As if it never happened.
> That's *love* for you.
> That's love for *you.*

I felt called to love like that. Given the quarter of a century since, in which I have professionally struggled with the church on the issue of homosexuality, I joke with friends about being a "professional victim." But in reality, and in my better moments, I have resisted living or acting as a victim. "Living well is the best revenge," the saying goes. I believe rather that rising above the need for vengeance is living well.

In this sense, the Reverend Richard Hetz lived well. Dick began worshiping with us at West Hollywood Presbyterian Church shortly after I arrived. Though he shared kinship with Ross Greek in believing that the church was called to address social injustice, he was Ross's opposite in the great pleasure he took in celebrating life as sacrament and in his deep reverence for celebrating sacramental life. He gave the finest dinner parties of anyone in the church: gourmet dishes accompanied by carefully selected wines and liqueurs, with a good and nonelitist mix of guests. Everyone in the church was invited to his annual "white elephant" champagne party between Christmas and New Year's, where we had great fun taking turns selecting either an already chosen and opened bizarre gift or one that was still wrapped. Dick's modest but artfully decorated home, replete with paintings by one of his two sons, was always open to friends and family.

Dick treated the sacred space of our sanctuary with the same care and regard. His initial service to the church was arranging flowers or blossoms in the chancel, cut from his own garden or trees. For palms on Palm Sunday, he "assisted" highway maintenance crews by pruning low palm trees along freeway on-ramps. He created handsome pedestals and containers for these natural creations. He brought in tasteful, special decorations, depending on the season, from Advent wreaths and garlands to black draping for the cross and Communion table during Lent.

We gradually learned Dick's story. He was gay, but of a generation that had felt compelled to marry. His wife struggled with mental illness. He had served several congregations as pastor. Twenty years before we met, he had been entrapped by a police officer who had picked him up in a gay bar, only to arrest him as soon as they went outside. The scandal forced him to leave the congregation that he served, and the presbytery ordered psychiatric care but otherwise hardly lifted a pastoral finger to help. Ross was the exception, serving as a support for Dick during this bleak time. Dick felt compelled to leave active ministry and became a salesman in a Beverly Hills office furniture store.

Despite treatment, Dick's wife became worse, and eventually took her own life, hanging herself while their sons were at school. Her family did not fault Dick, and remained closer to him in the years that followed than his own family did. Both of his sons turned out to be gay. The son who was an artist developed cancer in his late twenties and Dick cared for him until he died. All of this happened in the house in which we frequently enjoyed Dick's hospitality. When I first met this gracious and gentle, loving and joyful man, I could never have imagined that his life had included so much tragedy. He did not waste his life with blaming or faulting God, the church, or anyone. He endured and enjoyed.

When Ross Greek reluctantly retired, some of us hoped Dick would return to the ministry as pastor of our congregation. Through benign neglect, the Presbyterian Church had never taken away Dick's ordination. But Dick insisted that I was his pastor. So we struck an agreement: he would do the things I could not do, being unordained, such as moderate the Session (the board of elders of a local Presbyterian church) and celebrate the sacraments of Baptism and Communion, and I would take care of everything else. The arrangement worked beautifully. Especially when celebrating Communion, Dick brought an authentic reverence to the sacrament that only someone of his age, personal experience, and deep spirituality could have provided.

One evening, Dick invited someone he had just met home for dinner. He used his finest china, crystal, and silverware. But after dessert, the man took out a gun, tied Dick up, and demanded all of his valuables. Dick complied, but the man slit his throat, and, because he was not dying "fast enough," shot him in the head and set the house afire, escaping in Dick's car.

Our congregation was devastated. After the funeral, as the

grief wore off among church members, anger took its place. But strangely, it was not anger at the murderer, who had been apprehended. Indeed, Dick's remaining son, who would tragically die himself of a chance blood infection a few years later, joined us in petitioning the judge that the convicted murderer not be given the death penalty, because Dick himself opposed capital punishment. Rather than scapegoating a suspect who appeared to have no conscience, church members felt rage at the church's earlier scapegoating of Dick. In their view, the murderer had only completed the unnecessary sacrifice initiated by the church's original excommunication. As I wrote in chapter 5, people who kill or attack gays frequently offer religious justification. The original violence to Dick's character and life was laid at the feet of the Presbyterian Church.[1]

In order to help vent the parishioners' rage in a constructive way, I encouraged each church member to select a leader in our presbytery and write a letter to that person, explaining their feelings and telling their own stories. Then, with money generated in memory of Dick, we mailed copies of John Boswell's *Christianity, Social Tolerance, and Homosexuality* to all senior pastors of churches in the presbytery. One church that Dick served, not the one that dismissed him, became a More Light congregation (a Presbyterian church that welcomes lesbians and gays into full membership) in honor of their former pastor, and created a memorial garden in his name. Subsequently its pastor, the Reverend Donn Crail, became the third director of the Lazarus Project.

Significantly, our own church's final tribute to Dick was to commission the design and construction of a larger Communion

---

1. When confronted with the meaninglessness of such violence, many of us try to find sacred purpose hidden within it: "It was God's will," or "God had a purpose unknown to us." While this way of thinking is understandable, I believe it is nonetheless heretical, for it is claiming violence as sacred and proclaiming that God desires violence. This religious understanding is precisely what we must challenge. The congregation did not believe that the violence done either to Dick's livelihood (his loss of church vocation) or to his life (his murder) was divinely inspired. Their own vulnerability expressed in grief and anger manifested itself in meaningful, sacred actions. But that does not, in my view, render the violence done to Dick sacred or meaningful. To give another example: there is nothing good or godly about AIDS. Yet our positive response to the pandemic by helping people living with HIV/AIDS individually and institutionally is godly and holy and sacred. The violence of the disease is not made good or sacred by our sacramental responses. Neither is the violence of Jesus' death made good or sacred by the sacrament of Communion.

table dedicated in his memory. On this table sits a wooden chalice, given me by my first Christian boyfriend, who has since died of AIDS, and a wooden bread plate, given me by Dick to match the chalice. Carved on the chancel side of the table are the words, "In loving memory of Rev. Richard H. Hetz, 1919–1983." On the side facing the congregation is Jesus' imperative to his disciples, "This do in remembrance of me."

In the words of the parishioners' letters and Boswell's book, and in the sacrament of Communion, we tried to find meaning in the face of the meaningless violence that had taken our friend. But the violence had no sacred meaning. Dick's life had sacred meaning. As time passed, Dick's saintly qualities grew in our memory and his human limitations diminished. Communion meant more to us, and some of us continued to toast him during congenial dinners or parties, either aloud or in our hearts. A saint is believed to serve as a sacrament of Christ's continuing presence. Dick Hetz fulfilled that calling with us in a life well lived despite tragedy.

UNDOING THE SCAPEGOAT MECHANISM

Living well is living without vengeance, without returning violence for violence, without employing the scapegoat mechanism. Jesus taught this and, remarkably, the disciples got this. Though his crucifixion was laid at the feet of both religious and political authorities, there is never any indication that Jesus' disciples plotted revenge. Rather, they prayed and preached and practiced their faith for the conversion of the marginalized and the oppressor alike. Jesus had preached repentance, for the commonwealth of God was at hand, and his disciples lived this vision, living well—communally, sharing possessions, distributing to the needy, being inclusive of anyone who confessed faith in Jesus. The sacraments gave them glimpses of that vision, that commonwealth, past, present, and future. In a way, they "toasted Jesus" at their shared meals, remembering his Last Supper with them, and this evolved into what we call the Eucharist or Holy Communion. In so doing they also "remembered the future" that Jesus promised when he told them he would drink again with them in the commonwealth of God.

There has always been debate about whether Jesus' final meal with his disciples was a Passover Seder or a friendship meal, such as a rabbi would have with followers. The Synoptic Gospels imply it was a Passover meal, but John's Gospel places it on the previous evening, and biblical scholars feel this makes more sense, since Jesus was crucified on the next day, and, if the Romans chose not to offend the Jews, he would not have been crucified on the day of a religious feast. (Remember, the Jewish day runs from dusk to dusk, and crucifixion was a Roman execution; stoning would have been the Jewish form of execution.) However, John's intent may have been simply to draw a parallel between Jesus and the lamb to be slain in preparation for the Passover—neither's bones were broken (John 19:36; Exodus 12:46).

What we know for sure is that Jesus introduced a new covenant that contrasted with former covenants that the Israelites had enjoyed with Yahweh, especially the Mosaic covenant, which grew out of their liberation from Egypt, was celebrated at Passover time, and gave them the law, celebrated fifty days later at Pentecost. There are two different traditions of the effecting of the Mosaic covenant as well. In one, Moses and other representatives of the Hebrews meet God for a holy meal on top of Mount Sinai, a meal that seals the covenant with no conditions (Exodus 24:1–2, 9–11). In the other, a sacrifice at the base of the mountain seals the covenant, and God promises to be with the Israelites if they obey God's law (Exodus 24:3–8). "Sealing" a covenant, in effect, transmutes it to an eternal, immutable realm. That both traditions are preserved suggests that each represents a dimension of the Israelites' experience of the covenant. In other words, both are "true" in a mythological rather than literal sense.

The same could be said of Jesus' Last Supper. The two different ways of understanding it mythologically present two aspects of the same reality: from one perspective, it was the Passover meal in which the innocent lamb that was slain is Jesus; from another, it was an agape feast of the communion of the saints that anticipates reunion with Christ. The former tends to be emphasized in the celebration of the Eucharist, in which the sacrifice is reenacted; the latter tends to be emphasized in Holy Communion, in which our unity in and with and through Christ is proclaimed. I use the phrase *tends to be emphasized* because, in reality today, either version of the sacrament does both: both the Eucharist and Communion for most Christians today represent both the sacrifice of Christ and our union with and in and through Christ.

We must distinguish between sacrifice and the crucifixion, between vulnerability and violence. While the disciples were eating, scripture tells us,

> Jesus took a loaf of bread, and after blessing it he broke it, gave it to the disciples, and said, "Take, eat; this is my body." Then he took a cup, and after giving thanks he gave it to them, saying, "Drink from it, all of you; for this is my blood of the covenant, which is poured out for many for the forgiveness of sins. I tell you, I will never again drink of this fruit of the vine until that day when I drink it new with you in my Father's kingdom." (Matthew 26:26–29)

Sharing a meal was already invested with feelings of intimacy and a sense of sacrament in Jesus' time and culture. After three years of ministry together, it would mean all the more. Add to this Jesus' explicit language of offering himself and a new covenant in this bread and this wine, and already we have a sacrificial offering, already we have vulnerability. When Jesus prayed later in the garden of Gethsemane for God's will, not his, to be done, we may understand Jesus' and God's will as aligned not for violence, but rather to meet violence with vulnerability, refusing to change the divine nature or essence present in Jesus (and *already* offered to his disciples *before* the crucifixion) into something other than it was: love. This love does not insist on its own way; it is persuasive rather than coercive, transforming rather than conforming. A covenant of love that was "sealed"—transmuted into the eternal realm, into permanence, by Jesus' final acts of vulnerability in offering himself in a meal and on the cross, just as the Mosaic covenant was sealed in one tradition by a meal and in another by a sacrifice.

Just as a sacrificed animal would have been eaten by the priests of the temple, Jesus offers his body and blood to the priesthood of all believers. He gives us his embodiment as preparation for the

Spirit he would later send (in John this comes directly from the breath of the risen Christ [John 20:22]; in Acts the Spirit descends in power at Pentecost after Christ's ascension [Acts 2:1–4]). Because of their ritual eating of his body and blood, early Christians were accused of cannibalism. The spiritual significance of cannibalism is that at least some cannibals ritually ingest the part of the body invested with the virtue of the sacrificial victim they wish to incarnate. The disciples wished to ingest, to embody, to incarnate Jesus' virtues, and so they symbolically ate his body and blood, thus participating in the divine life. This practice paralleled that of Hellenistic religious cults of Jesus' day in which a common meal enabled participants to enter into the life of a deity.

Possibly the first openly gay activist at Union Theological Seminary in New York City, the late Reverend Howard Wells, gave me this idea. He had fallen in love with someone who soon abandoned him, leaving him emotionally desolate. He came to realize that what he had experienced was not love, which would not have wanted to possess the beloved as desperately as he did, but rather, infatuation. Infatuation, he came to believe, was *wanting* the other person—wanting within oneself something about that person. He realized that to get beyond his infatuation, he needed to incorporate the virtues of the beloved that he desired. Many of us have experienced the wisdom of becoming the person we are looking for in our quest for a lover. Howard saw a metaphorical connection between his experience and that of Christ's disciples. The disciples wanted to incorporate the virtues of their beloved Christ. This is what René Girard calls "good mimesis" in the sense that they wished to emulate Jesus, not take his place, in their "imitation of Christ." "Bad mimesis" would have been if they themselves had sacrificed Jesus to gain his attributes; rather, he offered himself to them.[2] Whatever "transaction" took place culminated in the Last Supper, *before* the crucifixion.

Part of our own good mimesis means a refusal, with Christ, to

---

2. *Though there appeared to have been multiple motivations behind the religious leaders' desire to do away with Jesus, at least one aspect of their destructive passion may have been "bad mimesis," since they are often depicted as jealous of Jesus' authority by which he spoke to the people and of the esteem with which the people held him. Bad mimesis may have prompted Judas's betrayal, too, but we cannot know this, since there is only speculation about his motives.*

scapegoat others as we are scapegoated, or to return violence for violence. When one of his disciples drew his sword and cut off the ear of the high priest's slave who had come to arrest Jesus, Jesus responded, "Put your sword back in its place; for all who take the sword will perish by the sword. Do you think that I cannot appeal to my Father, and he will at once send me more than twelve legions of angels?" (Matthew 26:52–53). Jesus wanted nothing to do with vengeance and retributive violence. Notice that the disciple cuts off the ear of a slave, another marginalized scapegoat. One of the ways oppressors have their way is by setting the oppressed at odds with one another.

The very nature of the scapegoat mechanism blinds us as to who our scapegoats are, according to Girard. The power of Jesus in undoing the scapegoat mechanism is that he opens the eyes of people of faith to the truth that the victim rather than the perpetrator of the sacrificial system is *God*. Thus Jesus gives vision to the blind man, while Pharisees who think they see are instead blind to their intended victim (John 9). Thus *we* understand that our government and our religious institutions are scapegoating us, while they suffer under the delusion that they are defending traditional family values.

Historically, similar delusions have rendered religions among the most violent human institutions, of which the crusades, inquisitions, and "holy" wars are prominent examples. If only Christianity had gotten the anti-scapegoat message of the gospel! Supposed sacred violence at the heart of its gospel made violence against "heretics" and "infidels" tenable. Not who goes into the church, but what comes out of the church's heart is what defiles it, to paraphrase Jesus (see Mark 7:14–23).

It is easier to see others' scapegoats. As Jesus put it, "Why do you see the speck in your neighbor's eye, but do not notice the log in your own eye?" (Matthew 7:3). As observers, it is easier for us to discern: The scapegoating of Jews in Europe led them to Israel, where Jews and Palestinians scapegoat one another. Anglo-European Americans have scapegoated African Americans, who then scapegoated American Jews who owned shops in their ghettos, and now scapegoat Korean Americans for much the same reason. All races scapegoat one another. Males scapegoated women as inferior and immoral; now, when sensitized to their scapegoating, women sometimes scapegoat males as well as women who choose "traditional" roles. Children scapegoated by abuse or molestation sometimes become adults who scapegoat their own children in the same way. And it often feels like *every* group scapegoats gays and lesbians!

How then do we determine our own scapegoats in the lesbian and gay community? We may listen for them to tell us, and, because most of us belong to more than one category of persons, we may simply listen to one another. Like other minorities, we often experience what is called "lateral" or "horizontal" violence, that is, directing our hostilities toward one another rather than at systems that oppress us. As mentioned earlier, we scapegoat our own leaders. We scapegoat the opposite gender. We scapegoat other races, particularly minorities. We scapegoat bisexuals and the transgendered. We scapegoat those on either side of the closet door. We scapegoat any of us who fulfill stereotypes and caricatures. We scapegoat by age or appearance. We scapegoat people with HIV, who sometimes scapegoat those without. In relation to HIV/AIDS, we scapegoat the medical profession and the government (though it is also true that we must challenge them as well as ourselves). We scapegoat our own sexual minorities: leather folk, drag queens, the fetish groups, the body beautiful gang, the singles crowd, the recreational sex folk, the opposite-gender married types, the same-gender married types, and so on. It is because of them we are not getting accepted, we say. Or it is because of them that we are getting mainstreamed, losing our edge, we say. They have employed the wrong strategy. They are not helping. They are an embarrassment to the community. They are too militant. They have divided the community. Etcetera.

As a religious gay person, however, I must say that the group we dump on most is the religious community. Now I need to offer a caveat here, like, "Just because you're paranoid doesn't mean they're not out to get you." The religious community has unprovidentially served as among the most likely to scapegoat us, whether in congregations or in the culture by pushing anti-gay legislation.

Even denominations that supposedly support our civil rights wimp out when it comes to matching the efforts of the religious right, or indeed, simply the conservative wing of their own communions. As spiritually abused children of religion, we have much right to our rage and our fear.

Having said that, I must also say that our fears often become phobic and our rage becomes rabid and violent when it comes to religion, more so than with any other source of oppression. Just consult with gay religious groups and you will find that they have felt ignored, maligned, attacked, and ridiculed by "their own" gay and lesbian community for maintaining their faith and their association with our "greatest" oppressor. I like to point out that my secularized lesbian sisters and gay brothers frequently ask me why I stay in the church, while few of them have ever considered leaving the United States, whose government and system of laws is the single largest oppressor of our people in this country! John Boswell told me that he was stunned when the most hostile reaction to his book *Christianity, Social Tolerance, and Homosexuality* came from the gay press, who somehow viewed it as an "apologetic" for the church, when his intent was to help the church understand that its current anti-gay sentiment is not inherently Christian nor has it always been a component of Christian tradition.

Avoiding the tendency to scapegoat, to resist rendering violence for violence, is not about refusing to hold our oppressors accountable. Not long ago my denomination approved an anti-gay amendment to our church constitution. In our gay-affirming congregation that Sunday, my lover expressed grief that the church could do such a thing. Immediately came the response from several people, including a gay man, "We must 'forgive them, for they know not what they do.'" My lover felt that his feelings were dismissed. He told me afterward, "The issue became about my lack of forgiveness rather than the church's lack of inclusion." It is true that Jesus extended mercy from the cross for those who did not realize they were participating in scapegoating, but only after he denounced the scribes and Pharisees and their system of sacrifice and scapegoating that would put him there:

Woe to you, scribes and Pharisees, hypocrites! For you build the
tombs of the prophets and decorate the graves of the righteous,
and you say, "If we had lived in the days of our ancestors, we
would not have taken part with them in shedding the blood of
the prophets." Thus you testify against yourselves that you are
descendants of those who murdered the prophets. Fill up, then,
the measure of your ancestors. You snakes, you brood of vipers!
How can you escape being sentenced to hell? Therefore I send
you prophets, sages, and scribes, some of whom you will kill
and crucify, and some you will flog in your synagogues and pur-
sue from town to town, so that upon you may come all the righteous blood shed on earth, from the blood of righteous Abel to
the blood of Zechariah son of Barachiah, whom you murdered
between the sanctuary and the altar. Truly I tell you, all this will
come upon this generation. (Matthew 23:29–36)

I do not think that Jesus would have liked to have his later words
on forgiveness thrown up at him in this context. Nonetheless, immediately following this passage Jesus switched from justifiable
rage to loving lament:

Jerusalem, Jerusalem, the city that kills the prophets and stones
those who are sent to it! How often have I desired to gather your
children together as a hen gathers her brood under her wings, and
you were not willing! See, your house is left to you desolate. For
I tell you, you will not see me again until you say, "Blessed is the
one who comes in the name of the Lord." (Matthew 23:37–39)

When it comes to the matter of forgiveness of our opposition, I
confess to mixed feelings. Frankly, I take great comfort in the Nazi
hunters of our time who, half a century after the fact, still search
out Nazi war criminals to place them on trial for the *shoah* perpetrated against Jews, gypsies, gay people, Seventh-Day Adventists,
and political dissidents. I take comfort because I think that, in the
future, our posterity might similarly seek out those who abused
and oppressed us and bring them to justice. Yet at the same time,
I am not sure I would want to spend my life caught up in recrimi-
nation and retributive justice. I am not sure how spiritually healthy
that would be for me.

Jesus said,

> You have heard that it was said, "An eye for an eye and a tooth for a tooth." But I say to you, Do not resist an evildoer. But if anyone strikes you on the right cheek, turn the other also; and if anyone wants to sue you and take your coat, give your cloak as well; and if anyone forces you to go one mile, go also the second mile. (Matthew 5:38–41)

Remember Paul's parallel attitude in Romans in which he quotes from his Jewish tradition in Deuteronomy 32:35 and Proverbs 25:21–22:

> Beloved, never avenge yourselves, but leave room for the wrath of God; for it is written, "Vengeance is mine, I will repay, says the Lord." No, "if your enemies are hungry, feed them; if they are thirsty, give them something to drink; for by doing this you will heap burning coals on their heads." [This is an idiom that means, "make them feel ashamed."] Do not be overcome by evil, but overcome evil with good. (Romans 12:19–21)

These passages from Jesus and Paul mean to imply not that we must cooperate with evil, but rather that we do not retaliate evil for evil. This ideal is being exercised as I write these words by South Africa's Truth and Reconciliation Commission headed by Bishop Desmond Tutu. Those who perpetrated atrocities during apartheid are being invited to admit them publicly with no fear of retribution. This airing of the national wounds seems preferable to the secrets and lies that would cover up the devastation of white rule and apartheid in the former South Africa. The new government's resistance to scapegoating is also evident in that South Africa is the first nation in the world to specifically protect the rights of lesbians and gay men in its constitution.

Previously I described our spiritual abuse. In the cycle of abuse, those who abuse others are often those who have been abused. We must remember that our spiritual abusers may be victims of spiritual abuse themselves. To them, spirituality may have more to do with power and authority, control and conformity than with communicating and receiving grace and love. Some of us may have once embraced such an understanding of spirituality to control our own sexuality. Even now, coming into a positive identity, some of us may want to practice a spirituality that has more to do with control than grace. While confronting and challenging those who practice spiritual abuse, *all* victims of spiritual abuse need compassion and forgiveness. In their own spiritual sensitivity, our abusers also need to be reached out to with tender, loving care.

One rural pastor of a congregation of the United Church of Christ in Iowa pointed out that the church was shifting from declaring homosexuality a sin to proclaiming it a gift. "But," he asked, "where's the repentance?" Where is the church's repentance for being wrong in the past, for destroying our lives and relationships? I wonder about that too. South Africa's reconciling program has no requirement for "confession" or "repentance," simply of telling the truth. Is that really enough?

At least it is a start. If we are to unmask the sacrificial system, to reveal the spiritual bankruptcy of scapegoating and of violence, telling the truth goes a long way toward undoing a pattern of human culture and religion that puts someone like Jesus on a cross. In the context of a naked God on the cross crucified by those God created and loved and blessed and chose and called, the words "Forgive them, for they know not what they do!" should prompt us mere humans to come out of reciprocal vengeance and violence.

LARGER-THAN-LIFE FAITH

What got Jesus to this point? What empowered him to be so beneficent that he could extend forgiveness to those who had no idea of the evil that they were doing? In the PBS series *The Power of Myth,* Joseph Campbell claimed that Jesus, like other sacrificial victims who went happily to their fate, was aware of his own myth—the larger-than-life meaning of his own life and death. That may be true, but it also may simply be that Jesus had faith that God's purpose was working itself out in whatever he was about to endure. In other words, he was aware of God's larger-than-life purpose for *every* life, every person's myth. Regardless, Campbell quotes the apocryphal Christian Acts of John, which depicts a more detailed conclusion to the Last Supper than the Gospels of Mark and Matthew, which say simply, "When they had sung the hymn, they went out to the Mount of Olives" (Mark 14:26; Matthew 26:30). In the Acts of John, Jesus said to the disciples, "Let us dance!" They began circling around Jesus, holding hands, antiphonally singing "Amen!" to each of the following phrases from Jesus:

> Glory be to thee, Father.
> Glory be to thee, Word!
> I would be born and I would bear!
> I would eat and I would be eaten!
> Thou that dancest, see what I do, for thine is this passion of
>   [personhood], which I am about to suffer!
> I would flee and I would stay!
> I would be united and I would unite!
> A door am I to thee that knocketh at me. . . .
> A way I am to thee, a wayfarer.

If Jesus and his disciples were sharing the Passover meal, the hymn assigned to close the meal then would have been Psalms 115 and 118, which are no less mythical:

> Not to us, O LORD, not to us, but to your name give
>   glory,
>   for the sake of your steadfast love and your
>   faithfulness. (115:1)
> I thank you that you have answered me
>   and have become my salvation.
> The stone that the builders rejected
>   has become the chief cornerstone.
> This is the LORD's doing;
>   it is marvelous in our eyes.
> This is the day that the LORD has made;
>   let us rejoice and be glad in it.
> Save us, we beseech you, O LORD!
>   O LORD, we beseech you, give us success!
> Blessed is the one who comes in the name of the LORD.
>   (118:21–26)

I believe that Jesus had larger-than-life faith in his being called out, which is not to say he did not also have doubt. But he had faith in his calling to reveal God and God's love and hope and promise for us. He did not know how things would turn out, but he trusted God. (One could say similar things of the great proponents of nonviolence in the twentieth century, Mahatma Gandhi, the Reverend Martin Luther King Jr., Dorothy Day, and César Chavez.) To use Søren Kierkegaard's phrase, Jesus made "a leap of faith." His faith both enabled him to take that leap and ennobled him to offer forgiveness.

Though it might be presumptuous to imagine that each of our separate leaps of faith in coming out carries mythic weight, I believe that the more we become aware of how *collectively* our coming out is yet another movement of the Holy Spirit in the world, the bolder we will be and become to trust God and forgive our opponents, *because we will trust our own myth,* our own sense of our sacred purpose as called-out ones. When we forgive our opponents, they are unable to spiritually wound us further. As Henri Nouwen said:

> When you let your wounded self express itself in the form of apologies, arguments, or complaints—through which it cannot be truly heard—you will only grow frustrated and increasingly feel rejected. Claim the God in you, and let God speak words of forgiveness, healing, and reconciliation, words calling to obedience, radical commitment, and service.
>
> People will constantly try to hook your wounded self. They will point out your needs, your character defects, your limitations and sins. That is how they attempt to dismiss what God, through you, is saying to them.[2]

Nouwen wrote these words ten years ago in a personal journal, while struggling with an unrequited love. The journal, *The Inner Voice of Love,* was finally published in 1996, released on the very day that his heart gave out. As usual, Henri speaks to more than just himself. He speaks to you and to me in our own endeavor to claim the God in us and to proclaim God's gospel as we struggle with the unrequited love of the church. They know not what they do, they know not the message they miss.

---

2. *Henri J. M. Nouwen,* The Inner Voice of Love *(New York: Doubleday & Co., 1996), 99.*

Our Christian brothers and sisters find things wrong with us and our community so they may avoid listening to their own inner voice of love, the voice that hungers for intimate, affectionate, and yes, even grasping touch. We have touched too much, they say, been too intimate with too many people or are too open about our intimacy. Thus they hook us in our vulnerability. Yet our vulnerability is our strength, for therein lies the message of both creation and Creator. Touch is required to create, to redeem, to heal, and to inspire. From the shaping of human flesh to the laying on of hands, God's word does not return empty, but returns with the lover embraced.

We apologize. We argue. We lament. They cannot hear us. They shut down. They do not listen. They run away. I invited a friendly member of our opposition to engage in a written dialogue in book form, but he refused, explaining *gentlemanly* that it would give credibility to our side. Did he not understand the *mutual* vulnerability at stake?

I believe it is time to stop apologizing, stop arguing, stop lamenting. It is time to stop speaking out of our wounded selves. It is time to speak from our center where God has set up house, offers us communion, and gives us a message to deliver to the church.

The message is far more revolutionary and radical (yes, *both*) than the mere acceptance of lesbian, gay, bisexual, and transgendered persons, even more so than celebrating our ministries and marriages. The message is that God loves all of us more deeply than we have imagined, allowed, or celebrated. God loves us deep in our genitals, in our nipples, in all our pleasure sites. God loves us in all places, times, circumstances, and conditions. God loves us without condition or even expectation, although we know the inevitable transformation that occurs in us when we are the beloved.

Let others quibble over rituals and laws and theology and the Bible. We know that all ritual, all laws, all theology, and all of the Bible have been created for us, not us for them—just like the sabbath. Let us proclaim "words of forgiveness, healing, and reconciliation, words calling to obedience, radical commitment, and service." Then, more clearly than ever, it will be God's word that the church resists.

In understanding our collective myth, in comprehending the

essence of our gospel, we can move beyond our woundedness to celebrate the ultimate outcome of our coming out. As the resurrected Jesus was made known to the disciples on the road to Emmaus "in the breaking of bread," we are made known to others in the breaking of the silence regarding sexuality and spirituality. Just as God came to the victims of ritual sacrifice trying to heal their wounds and restore life, so God comes to us in our vulnerability to heal our wounds and renew our lives. God comes also to the Body of Christ, the church, in its own vulnerability and brokenness, to heal its divisions, just as God comes to the world, in its vulnerability and brokenness, to overcome its violence with peace.

I hope that our coming out will invite and welcome others to come out of whatever closets they endure. Our celebration of coming out is evangelical, proclaiming a new communion that is welcoming and inclusive. One day, on a long run, I ran past a church sign that listed the upcoming Sunday's sermon plus the fact that Communion would be offered. The title was, "The Bottom Line, an Idol." But as I ran past I mistakenly read: "The Bottom Line, an Idol Communion." I quickly realized my mistake, but I used it as fodder for thought during the remaining miles of my run. I pondered what an "idol Communion" would be. I thought of my friend Pat Hoffman's observation about a church committee on homosexuality. Its membership included no gays or lesbians, and its report spent a great deal of time describing how beautifully they got along, despite the controversial nature of their work. Pat said, "As Christians we get so caught up with ourselves and our warm and fuzzy feelings, that we fail to look around and see who's missing." An idol Communion, I thought, would be a Communion we idolized, mistaking a mere foretaste of God's commonwealth for the commonwealth itself.

The following Sunday, as I was offered Christ's broken body in a Communion service by an older gay man, denied his vocation of ministry, in many ways broken by the church, I realized that "an idol Communion" inevitably leads to "an idle Communion," that is, one that does not really enter into the brokenness of Christ, the experience of the victim and of the scapegoat.

In his Gospel, Matthew precedes the story of the Last Supper with a final parable of Jesus, that of the Last Judgment. In it, Jesus identifies himself with victims, and those who minister to them are the ones destined for glory: "I was hungry and you gave me food, I was thirsty and you gave me something to drink, I was a stranger and you welcomed me, I was naked and you gave me clothing, I was sick and you took care of me, I was in prison and you visited me" (Matthew 25:35–36).

Our celebration of coming out is incomplete until we serve as Christ to others victimized by the religious, political, and economic systems and structures of our world. Our celebration of coming out must become inclusive of all intended scapegoats. That is the message of Christ. That is the lesson learned by the Body of Christ in the various movements of the Spirit that opened the church's doors yet wider, from the inclusion of strangers at Pentecost and of Gentiles in Acts to the later Reformation and reformations of the church.

I began writing this chapter, appropriately enough, on Maundy Thursday, continued writing through Good Friday, and am concluding it on Holy Saturday of Holy Week. On Maundy Thursday, I participated in our church's Tenebrae liturgy. I was reluctant because my denomination had just ratified a law prohibiting my service to the church because I am in a same-gender covenant relationship, and I have been reevaluating my continuing participation in the church. One part of the Passion narrative especially captured my imagination. When Jesus was arrested, the disciples fled. It occurred to me that, in this anti-gay law, the religious leaders had once again arrested Jesus. If I am to be a faithful disciple, I cannot abandon Jesus to them. Nor can I, with Peter, deny him because of gay peer pressure of those gathered around the fire in the courtyard outside today's Sanhedrins.

In *The Church and the Sacraments*,[3] Karl Rahner described a sacrament as a visible means of grace that acts with the intensity of a magnifying glass, producing not only more light, but fire. As

---

3. *Karl Rahner*, The Church and the Sacraments *(London, 1963)*.

I await God outside the church's closet on the eve of Easter, I affirm my own belief that coming out is a sacrament, a visible means of grace that acts like a prism, transforming more light into a rainbow of promise for all who refuse to abandon the outcast.

7

Rites for the Soul

Early Christian converts were baptized and received their first Communion before the significance of either sacrament was explained to them. The belief behind this practice was that no one, not even a believer, could understand the meaning of a sacrament before experiencing it.

In Jesus Christ, Christians believe that God's Word became flesh. It is in relationship to this Incarnation, this "personing" of God, that we are converted, transformed, and sanctified as Christians.

Both of these dynamics are confirmed by our own experience of coming out as lesbian, gay, bisexual, transgendered, and as their family members, friends, and allies. Coming out is an experience best understood on the other side of the closet door—in other words, by those who have experienced it, like a sacrament. Coming out incarnates our reality: converting, transforming, and sanctifying all who believe in us, including ourselves. Thus coming out may help everyone involved to overcome fear, prejudice, and narrow-mindedness, just as, in a much more profound way, an encounter with Jesus causes *metanoia,* the New Testament Greek word for an *about-face,* a conversion experience.

Many of us have read books affirming our sacred worth, including this one. But our bodies, our guts, our souls have taken in so much spiritual abuse, so many negative messages from our church and culture, that our feelings and emotions and psyches and souls are well behind our minds in processing the truth of our belovedness. Our lovemaking has been so important to us because it alleviates the violence done to our souls by those who may not have known what they were doing in scapegoating us, in questioning our sacred worth. As a result, many of us have clung to sexual experience, to lovers, to gay ghettos and groups, desperately seeking healing for deep, spiritual wounds. In response to the violence done to us, a few of us have manifested violence in sexual expressions, relationships, and within

our community, just as those abused as children often become
abusers themselves. Others of us, numbed by continual and brutal rejection from church and society, have manifested an indifference in
sexual relationships that leads to exploitation. For those of us who
are taught that we are neither lovable nor capable of loving, this becomes a self-fulfilling prophecy. Some of us have held on to victimization as a source of identity, because having people feel sorry for
us is better than having them bash us. For those who have been humiliated by shame, taking abuse may seem easier than taking responsibility. Letting others take control may feel more natural than
taking charge of our own lives. It is remarkable that, despite the possibility of these unhealthy responses to unhealthy circumstances, the
majority of us manage healthy, loving relationships.

"Perfect love casts out all fear," 1 John 4:18 tells us. Perfect
love heals the spiritual abuse that causes us to fear that we are unworthy, unholy, unredeemed. But human love is seldom perfect,
not always accessible, nor capable of meeting every need. Thus,
though lovemaking and lovers go far toward healing our souls,
many of us have discerned that we need more. We need, in a sense,
to make love with God, the perfect Lover: we need to find physical, soulful ways to relate to God, because we carry wounds in-
flicted "in God's name" deep within our somatic consciousness.
Like Jacob, we wrestle with God, and we will not let God go until
God blesses us. Like Mary, we welcome union with God that
blesses the fruit of our wombs and our loins.

In our desire to touch or be touched by God, many of us have discovered sacramentals: material things that we experience as holy,
sacred, godly. Traditional sacramentals include candles, water, in-
cense, rosaries, pictures of saints or biblical scenes, Bibles and
hymnals, icons, stained-glass windows, stations of the cross, cruci-
fixes and crosses, altars, and church architecture. Nontraditional
sacramentals might include nature, trees, flowers, stones, crystals,
animals, photographs of loved ones, tokens given us by loved ones,
a view from a window or deck, a place to think, a peaceful location.
The Reverend Janie Spahr sometimes brings items to her speaking
engagements that have been given her by a variety of people: a

friend with AIDS, a grandmother of a lesbian granddaughter, a gay couple she married, a congregation that welcomes lesbians and gay men, and so on. She passes her sacramentals around the room for everyone to see, touch, and smell, thus connecting them to some sacred aspect of the giver whose story is included in the presentation.

In our homes, offices, or study cubicles, we each might find sacramentals we already have without necessarily realizing their sacred purpose. We might consider their meaning, what memories—perhaps stories—they offer, the people to whom they connect us, and how they remind us of the spiritual and sacred in our lives. We may hold them, look them over carefully, maybe even sniff or taste them. If we have not already done so, we could arrange them on a desk, computer, wall, bookshelf, mantel, file cabinet, or table to create a sacred space in which to meditate, pray, work, read, or make love.

As a community, we have created our own sacramentals: the pink triangle, the rainbow flag, and the AIDS Quilt all carry a profound sacred meaning that unites us against injustice, celebrates our diversity, and remembers those who have gone before us. Groups within our community have created sacramentals specific to their needs: Presbyterian gays and lesbians have the Shower of Stoles, commemorating the ministries of lesbian, gay, bisexual, and transgendered people; gay Mormons have just begun a Handkerchief Project, writing their stories on handkerchiefs symbolizing the pain of their excommunication (figuratively or in reality); the red ribbon for AIDS and pink ribbon for breast cancer keep before us two major health problems that our community suffers; the white ribbon worn by many reminds us of how many of our young people commit suicide. Even our buttons, pins, awards, and bumper stickers may have spiritual significance.

Devising our own rituals, our own sacramental rites, may be another path toward restoring our souls. Rituals engage our bodies in a way merely reading a book does not. Like sacramentals, rituals serve to remind us that the sacred is manifest in physical realities. As discussed earlier, spirituality is not merely something we think or read or speak about. Spirituality is also something we do and feel, eat and drink, taste and smell. Moreover, spirituality is something we do with others. Even when we are praying alone, we do so as part of a host of people across the globe directing their thoughts, words, and feelings toward the sacred, toward God.

The seven rituals included in this chapter are intended to challenge and transform those very things that have been literally *incorporated* in us that try to separate us from the love of God. It would claim too much to call them sacraments, but they may nonetheless serve sacramentally for those who experience in them a revelation of the sacred in themselves and among others. With a group that we gather or to which we already belong, these rituals could be used as they are or adapted to specific needs. They may be added to or blended into a regular service of worship, and permission is hereby granted for their use in worship with attribution. If no group or partner is available, we may read them aloud to ourselves, performing the required actions as celebrant, participant, and recipient, remembering that we are nonetheless a part of others also observing the ritual.

In the liturgies themselves, the lines in regular type may be spoken by a leader (a group may choose to have coleaders, or, better yet, pass the leadership around the circle) and those in bold type by the congregation, or the two types may be read antiphonally (choir and congregation, or left side and right side). Those who are the focus of the rite, may be designated by *N.,* which means that her/his first name is to be used. Instructions are in parentheses and italicized. The liturgies are designed so they may be used by Christians regardless of denomination or tradition. They include:

> Biblical Affirmations: Blessing One Another
> Coming Out: A Witness to the Resurrection
> A Call to Repentance: Confessing Homophobia and Heterosexism
> Turning the Tables: A Ritual of Anger and Grief
> Embracing Our Cause: A Ritual of Commitment to Justice
> Reclaiming Our Baptism: Turning the Church Upside Down
> Celebrating the Commonwealth: A Rite of God's Victory

Each of these seven rituals manifests a dimension of coming out. First we experience *affirmations* of our belovedness from one another and from our spiritual ancestors in the Bible. Thus we are empowered to *come out* to those who give us true sanctuary, our authentic spiritual community, whether it be a support group, a group of friends, or a congregation. Coming out calls us and our congregations and communities to *repent of homophobia and heterosexism.* We pause to *express our rage* ritually, lest it get the better of us and we express it violently. We *commit ourselves to justice,* and are commissioned as prophets to the world. We *reaffirm our baptism,* at the same time redefining our relationship with the church, choosing perhaps to be "in" but not "of" the church, choosing to leave a particular denomination, or choosing to leave the institutional church altogether in search of the church that cannot be contained in human structures. Finally, in a variation on Communion, we *celebrate glimpses and inbreakings of God's victory* and vision of a common spiritual wealth for us all, as well as the ultimate fulfillment of God's wish for humanity: a commonwealth of peace and prosperity for all.

BIBLICAL AFFIRMATIONS

Blessing One Another

The concept for this ritual came from John Bradshaw's PBS workshop series, *Healing the Shame That Binds You*. Small groups encircled a participant and offered affirmations the person should have heard the day she or he was born, like, "Welcome to the universe!" and "I'm so glad you're a girl!" or "I'm so glad you're a boy!" Watching this moving exercise, I realized that the same thing could be done using quotations from the Bible. Remember the character Pollyanna pointing out to her minister that there are more blessings than curses in scripture? Experiencing these blessings addressed personally to us dramatically restores our sense of sacred worth.

One may address the biblical affirmations that follow to oneself, or to others in pairs and in groups. In the latter two configurations, invite the recipient of the blessings to sit comfortably or kneel reverently in the center of those offering the affirmations. Give the recipient an opportunity to quiet the self, taking in deep and slow breaths, possibly closing eyes to distractions, becoming centered. Then, going around the circle, take turns offering the affirmations in the order printed here, with genuine feeling, inserting the recipient's first name. Pause briefly between each affirmation, so it can sink into the recipient's body and soul. Occasionally, but not every time, gently touch the person as you offer an affirmation. Check this out beforehand with each recipient; some may not feel comfortable being touched. On the final affirmation, the whole group may lay hands on the person. After the person has received every affirmation, give the recipient an opportunity to reflect silently for a moment or two before getting up to give the next recipient her or his place. Before any conversation, each person in the pair or group should have an opportunity to be the recipient. Then together, dialogue about what the exercise meant to each participant, first as receiver, then as giver of the affirmations. The group may want to conclude with a prayer, such as the prayer Jesus taught us, or a song.

The following verses are taken from the New Revised Standard Version unless otherwise noted, with language adapted for this purpose. The textual references are given for information only and should not be read aloud to the recipient.

"Let us make *N.* in our image, according to our likeness." . . . And God saw that *she/he* was very good. (*Genesis 1:26, 31*)

See, I have made you like God to Pharaoh. (*Exodus 7:1*)

N., choose life! (*Deuteronomy 30:19*)

What is *N.* that thou art mindful of *her/him?* Yet thou hast made *her/him* little less than God, and dost crown *her/him* with glory and honor. (*Psalm 8:4–5,* RSV)

Hail, O favored one, God is with you! Do not be afraid, *N.,* for you have found favor with God. (*Luke 1:28, 30,* RSV)

Blessed are you among *women/men,* and blessed is the fruit of your *womb/loins!* (*Luke 1:42*)

Do not be afraid, *N.;* for see—I am bringing you good news of great joy for all the people: to you is born this day a Savior. (*Luke 2:11*)

N. is my *daughter/son,* my Beloved, with whom I am well pleased. (*Matthew 3:17*)

Blessed are you, *N.,* for yours is the kingdom of heaven. (*Matthew 5:3*)

Therefore I tell you, *N.,* do not be anxious about your life. (*Matthew 6:25,* RSV)

For God so loved *N.,* that God gave *her/him* the Christ. (*John 3:16*)

N., you will know the truth, and the truth will make you free. (*John 8:32*)

N., God loved you with so much love that God was generous with mercy. God brought you to life with Christ. (*Ephesians 2:4,* JB)

N., you are God's work of art. (*Ephesians 2:10*, JB)

You are created in Christ Jesus to live the good life as from the beginning God intended you to live it. (*Ephesians 2:10*, JB)

I came that you, *N.*, may have life, and have it abundantly. (*John 10:10*)

I do not cease to give thanks for you, *N.*, as I remember you in my prayers. (*Ephesians 1:16*)

COMING OUT

A Witness to the Resurrection

The Communion table holds a loaf of bread, covered or tied by a strip of cloth (a rainbow flag may be used unless it is decided to tear the cloth), in turn covered and surrounded by stones (hymnals may be used as "stones"). People are called to gather around the table.

This ritual may be pluralized for several coming out at the same time or adapted for others who may wish to come out as parents, family, or friends of lesbian, gay, bisexual, or transgendered persons. It may also be adapted for persons living with HIV or AIDS.

Biblical quotations are adapted from the New Revised Standard Version of the Bible.

"N." is the name or names of those coming out. Alternative wording is indicated by slashes (/): choose one or more of the words as appropriate. Leadership may move around the circle; or it may be read by a choir or one side of the congregation. Bold print is read by either the whole congregation or the other side of the congregation. Italicized print in parentheses offers directions or explanations.

Leader: There is one body and one Spirit, just as you were called to the one hope of your calling, one Sovereign, one faith, one baptism, one God and Creator of all, who is above all and through all and in all. (*Ephesians 4:4*)

People: **God inspirits every soul, regardless of sexual orientation. God welcomes every body, though we may hide our nakedness. God hopes in every love, without partiality.**

Leader: According to the Gospel of John, Jesus was greatly disturbed in spirit to find his friend Lazarus dead and entombed. Christ called on faithful family members Mary and Martha as well as caring neighbors to roll the stone from the tomb and unbind the death cloths. Christ prayed to God, and called to Lazarus, "Come out!"

Leader (*Addresses the congregation*): Are you, family and neighbors, willing to remove the stone of prejudice that separates *N.* from full communion with the Body of Christ and with you?

People: **We are.**

Leader: Are you, family and neighbors, willing to undo the bonds that inhibit *N.* from the full, abundant life promised each one of us?

People: **We are.**

Leader: Are you, *N.*, willing to affirm death as a means to life, dying to your old self to accept your resurrected self, yet renouncing artificial forms of death, especially the closet that hides your light and your life?

N.: *I am.*

Leader: Are you, *N.*, willing to choose life, love, and liberation as a (lesbian/gay/bisexual/transgendered) Christian?

N.: *I am.*

Leader: Let us pray.

People: **Sacred God, bless *N.* and bless us all as we struggle with the stones of prejudice and the bonds of death. Lead us to choose life and enjoy love and liberate the oppressed in your name. Amen.**

Leader: Take away the stones.

(*Participants are requested to remove stones from the Communion table, naming them if they have names, such as "prejudice" or "legalism." Every stone must be removed, revealing a loaf of bread, wrapped in a strip of cloth.*)

Leader: Unbind *N.*, and let (*her/him*) go.

(*A preselected participant* [*spouse, lover, partner, family member, friend, pastor*] *removes the cloth from the bread and tears it in two, from top to bottom, just as the temple curtain separating*

the Holy of Holies was torn at Jesus' death [Mark 15:38]. Alter-
natively, the cloth could simply be unfolded or untied from the
bread. This would be the appropriate procedure if using the rain-
bow flag.)

Leader: Our risen Sovereign became known to the disciples on the
road to Emmaus in the breaking of bread, a sacrament of
God's offering of self. In like manner, our risen friend(s)
N. become(s) known to us in (*her/his/their*) own sacramental offering of (*herself/himself/themselves*), symbolized by this bread.

(Each one coming out takes a loaf or roll and everybody present
receives a piece of bread from her/him. For example, if three are
coming out, each recipient, including those who are coming out,
should receive three pieces of bread.)

(As each of those coming out gives a piece of bread to each per-
son, he/she says:)

N.: *I offer you the gift of myself.*

(The bread should be eaten as one receives. Receivers may offer
an appropriate response, such as a hug, a "thank-you," or an
"amen.")

(After all have eaten, the service continues:)

Leader: As Ruth pledged to Naomi, let us pledge to *N.:*
People: **We will never abandon you!**
Where you go, we will be there;
what is life to you will be vital for us.
Your people will be our own,
and your God will be our God.

> *(Ruth 1:16, adapted)*

(If more than one is coming out, pluralize the following:)

Leader: So then, *N.,* you are no longer a stranger or an alien, but
you are a citizen with the saints and also a member of the
household of God, built upon the foundation of the apostles and prophets, with Christ Jesus as the cornerstone.
(Ephesians 2:19–20)

N.:   *Thanks be to God!*

Leader: We are chosen, a royal priesthood, a holy nation, God's
own people, in order that we may proclaim the mighty
acts of God who called us out of shadows into God's mar-
velous light:

People: **Once we were not a people,**
but now we are God's people;
once we had not received mercy,
but now we have received grace.
(1 Peter 2:9–10)

Hymn "Amazing Grace"

*(You may choose to sing only the first verse. In any case, the fol-
lowing rewording is recommended for the first verse:)*

> Amazing Grace! How sweet the sound
> That saved a soul like me!
> I once was lost, but now am found,
> Was bound, but now I'm free!

Note: This ritual was written at the request of *Open Hands* and
published in the summer 1994 issue. This rite blends elements
from ancient sacraments—Baptism (renunciation of evil, affirmations of our call as a people and of our communal integrity) and
Communion (distribution of bread symbolic of sharing the self,
which is what God did in Christ). Coming out is a sacramental act

in which God is present in our vulnerability and by which we are "made new" as citizens of God's commonwealth.

There are also elements of other sacraments recognized by other Christians: Confirmation, because individuals coming out affirm their sexuality; Reconciliation, because the community names and removes the stones of prejudice; Ordination, because the call to diversity is affirmed; Marriage, because the community vows to the one coming out what Ruth vowed to Naomi; and "last rites," because this ritual recognizes the grief of letting go of a "past life" and yet also witnesses a resurrection to new life. (The subtitle "A Witness to the Resurrection" is used in some traditions for funerals.)

Thanks to the Reverend Woody Carey for suggesting the Emmaus image.

A CALL TO REPENTANCE

Confessing Homophobia and Heterosexism

Inspired by the vision of Lisa Larges

During the days of Nazi power in Germany, "undesirables" were systematically rounded up and placed in concentration camps, where most died of malnutrition and disease or were murdered. Each category of prisoner was given its own symbol to wear on their prison uniforms. Gay men were assigned pink triangles, and though German law overlooked lesbians, they too were sometimes referred to as "pink triangle people" in German society. (The three documented lesbians sent to concentration camps were incarcerated for other reasons.) When the Nazis were defeated at the end of World War II, gay people were the only concentration camp prisoners that were not liberated. Instead, they were sent to other prisons.

As worshipers enter or gather, they are each given a pink paper triangle to wear, which they should pin to their clothing. On the Communion table is a fire-resistant bowl, resting on a holder to absorb heat. Beside it is a lighted candle and a pestle for grinding. In the rear of the worship area are banners, which may include church logo or confessional banners (especially appropriate would be that of the Barmen Declaration), lesbian and gay religious group banners, and the rainbow flag.

The liturgy may be read responsively, possibly sharing leadership, or antiphonally.

Procession of Banners

(Banners are brought forward during singing of the hymn below, followed by worshipers, who gather around the table.)

Hymn   "Let All Mortal Flesh Show Reverence"

(Tune: Picardy. Words adapted from "Let All Mortal Flesh Keep Silence," the translation by Gerard Moultrie [1864] from the

Liturgy of St. James. Copyright © 1998 by Chris R. Glaser.
Permission granted for use in worship with attribution.)

Let all mortal flesh show reverence,
And in awe and wondrous delight
Ponder One born from among us
To inspire and to invite
Reconciliation: Christ, the Word of God,
Spoken to redeem, reunite.

Child of God, yet born of Mary,
That God's children all may be
One in faith and in baptism,
One in hope and charity;
One in Christ's flesh, and one in Christ's church,
Off'ring our diversity.

Alleluia! God comes among us,
Blessing us with human hands,
Loving us in earthly pleasures,
Leading us to take our stands
For God's healing love in our broken world,
For sweet justice in our lands.

Reading   Matthew 3:1–12

Reflections

*(Reflections may be inward and silent, or spoken [homily or
dialogue], sung, dramatized, danced, or omitted.)*

Leader: Repent! For the commonwealth of God is at hand!
People: **We confess that we have sinned in thought, word, and
deed, in acts of commission and omission, against our
lesbian sisters and gay brothers, and against our bisexual and transgendered sisters and brothers. Lamb
of God, who takes away the sins of the world, have
mercy on us.**

Leader: The Holocaust took the lives of the Rainbow people, forced to wear pink triangles, murdered in concentration camps, imprisoned even after others were liberated.

People: **We wear pink triangles as a symbol of our solidarity with them. Lamb of God, who takes away the sins of the world, have mercy on us.**

Leader: We burn the chaff of our prejudice, of our arrogance, of our ignorance, that prevented our repentance and caused our scapegoating and our wounding of lesbian and gay, bisexual and transgendered people.

People: **We burn the pink triangles as a symbol of our renouncing homophobia and heterosexism, as a symbol of our deliverance in Christ Jesus our Sovereign. Lamb of God, who takes away the sins of the world, grant us peace.**

(A leader lights the first triangle from the candle and places it in the bowl on the Communion table. Others place their triangles in one by one, to keep the fire going. If the fire dies, the candle may be used to ignite the next triangle. A reverent silence is observed until the flame dies. Then a leader grinds the ashes with the pestle. The bowl is passed.

Each person dips a finger in the ashes and makes the sign of the cross on her/his neighbor, saying:)

In Jesus Christ, you are forgiven.

Hymn   "Joy to the World!"

(Tune: Antioch. Words adapted from Isaac Watts [1719]. Copyright © 1998 by Chris R. Glaser. Permission granted for use in worship with attribution.)

> Joy to the world! God's Word is come:
> Let earth receive its grace;
> Let every heart
> Prepare it room—

Expand its warm embrace,
Expand its warm embrace,
Expand, expand God's warm embrace.

No more let walls divide our love,
Nor fear our hate require;
Christ comes to bless
Each covenantal rite
The gift of love inspires,
The gift of love inspires,
The gift, God's gift of love inspires.

Joy to the world!
The Savior calls
For mercy, truth, and grace,
So hope and trust
And faith may glow
In every child's face,
In every child's face,
In ev'ry, in ev'ry holy child's face.

TURNING THE TABLES

A Ritual of Anger and Grief

Cover the Communion table with ecclesiastical clutter, such as polity books, bylaws, position papers, minutes, reports, periodicals, church tabloids, and religious hate literature. In the baptismal font place figs or some other easy-to-handle fruit (cut up or whole), at least one piece for each participant.

The liturgy may be read responsively, possibly sharing leadership, or antiphonally.

Opening Sentences
(Adapted from Matthew 23)

Leader: My house shall be called a house of prayer for all peoples:

People: **But you have made it a den of thieves.**

Leader: Do not do as the Pharisees do, for they do not practice what they preach.

People: **They load heavy burdens, hard to bear, on the shoulders of others; but they themselves are unwilling to lift a finger to move them.**

Leader: They love to have places of honor, to be greeted with respect, and to have people call them reverend.

People: **But all who exalt themselves will be humbled, and all who humble themselves will be exalted.**

Leader: They lock people out of the commonwealth of God. They themselves do not enter, and when others do, they stop them.

People: **They cross sea and land to make a convert, and then make the new Christian twice the child of hell with burdensome demands.**

Leader: They tithe lightly, neglecting the weightier matters of the law: justice and mercy and faith.

People: **Woe to you, Pharisees, for you whitewash the church**

to look beautiful, but inside it is full of hypocrisy and
death.

Leader: Woe to you, Pharisees, for you dare to say, if you had
lived in the time of the prophets, you would have listened
to their words.

People: **But God sends you prophets today whom you reject
and exclude, spiritually killing them between the baptismal font and the altar.**

Leader: My church! My church!—The church that resists the
prophets and persecutes those sent to you: how often
Christ desired to gather you together as a hen gathering
her brood, and you refused!

People: **Your house of worship is left to you, desolate; for
you will not recognize us until you say,**

Unison: **Blessed are the ones who come in the name of the
Lord.**

Hymn   "O Blessed One, Come to Our Church Today"

*(Tune: Veni Emmanuel. Words adapted from "O Come, O Come,
Emmanuel," translation by John Mason Neale [1851] from an
anonymous c. 12th-century hymn. Adaptation Copyright © 1998
by Chris R. Glaser. Permission granted for use in worship with attribution.)*

> O Blessed One, come to our church today
> To clear a place within for us to pray;
> Gather us as hen does her brood:
> Those the church has poorly understood.
> Rejoice, rejoice, O blessed be the Name
> That welcomes us, whose gospel we proclaim.
>
> You shaped us each within a mother's womb,
> Although for us the world has no room;
> You formed our inward sighs, hopes, and dreams,

That our lives may discover what love means.
Rejoice, rejoice, O blessed be the Name
That welcomes us, whose gospel we proclaim.

We gather now in praise and in prayer—
Believing we will ever meet you there,
That you will never leave us alone;
Your steadfast love's eternally enthroned.
Rejoice, rejoice, O blessed be the Name
That welcomes us, whose gospel we proclaim.

Reading   Mark 11:12–25

Reflections

(*Reflections may be inward and silent, or spoken [homily or dialogue], sung, dramatized, danced, or omitted.*)

Clearing of the Temple
(*From Mark 11 and Isaiah 56*)

Leader: My house shall be called a house of prayer for all peoples:

People: **But you have made it a den of thieves.**

Leader: You have stolen from us our innocence, our sanctuary, our calling.

People: **You have cluttered Christ's table with ritual and legal obligations.**

Leader: Thus says our God: maintain justice, and do what is right,

People: **For soon my salvation will come, and my deliverance be revealed.**

Leader: Do not let the foreigner joined to the Sovereign say, "The Lord will surely separate me from God's people."

People: **And do not let the eunuch say, "I am just a dry tree."**

Leader: For these I will bring to my holy mountain, and make them joyful in my house of prayer,

People: **For my house shall be called a house of prayer for all peoples.**

Leader: Let us clear God's house!

(*Those aggrieved by a denomination's policy on homosexuality are invited to clear the ecclesiastical clutter off the table by sweeps of their hands, allowing it to fall to the floor. Then the leader proceeds:*)

Leader: Let us pray.
People: **Your table is bare, O God. Your fig tree, the church, resists feeding us, the Body of Christ.**
Leader: We lay our anger on the table.

(*Those closest to the table lay their fists on the table and keep them there.*)

Leader: We cry out our grief and despair.

(*Others lift open hands in the air and keep them there.*)

Leader: We shake our fist in a curse.

(*Still others shake a fist in the air above their heads. This is not intended for God, but for the fig tree that Jesus himself cursed.*)

Leader: My house shall be called a house of prayer for all peoples:
People: **But you have made it a den of thieves.**

(*Hands resume natural positions.*)

Leader: Jesus said:
People: **Have faith in God.**
Leader: Truly I tell you, if you say to this mountain, "Be taken up and thrown into the sea," and if you do not doubt in your heart, but believe that what you say will come to pass, it will be done for you.
People: **Have faith in God.**
Leader: So I tell you, whatever you ask for in prayer, believe that you have received, and it will be yours.

People: **O God, we believe, help our unbelief.**
Leader: Whenever you stand praying, forgive, if you have anything against anyone; so that your God in heaven may also forgive you your trespasses.
People: **O God, we forgive, help our unforgiveness.**
Leader: Have faith in God. Truly I tell you, if you say to this fig tree, "Be fruitful!" and do not doubt in your heart, but believe that what you say will come to pass, it will be done for you. Lift up your hands in blessing.

(*All lift their hands in blessing.*)

People: **Be fruitful! Be fruitful! Be fruitful!**
Leader: Let us enjoy the fruits of our baptism that the harvesters have rejected.

(*Pre-selected participants gather handfuls of figs from the baptismal font and place them on the Communion table.*)

Leader: Denied the bread and wine of full communion, we savor the fruits of the Spirit.

People: **The fruit of the Spirit is love, joy, peace, patience, kindness, generosity, faithfulness, gentleness, and self-control.** (*Galatians 5:22–23a*)
Leader: There is no law against such things. (*Galatians 5:23b*) Take, eat, these are the fruits of the Spirit. Taste and see that our God is good. (*Psalm 34:8*)

(*Everyone takes a fig or portion thereof and savors its taste.*)

Hymn   "Spirit of God, Rise Within My Heart"

(*Tune: Morecambe. "Spirit of God, Descend Upon My Heart"; new words Copyright © 1998 by Chris R. Glaser. Permission granted for use in worship with attribution.*)

Spirit of God, rise within my heart:
Spring from this earth, through all this beauty flow;
Strengthen my purpose, mighty as thou art,
And help me love earth with my body and soul.

Spirit of God, lead us to promised lands:
Reign with us now in all our wandering;
Give us the patience, bless our earthly hands
That we of Christ's love may make offering.

Spirit of God, O help us now discern
Where you are found, and whom you send to lead;
Send us your Passion so that we may yearn
To bring forth fruit to feed all those in need.

Spirit of God, O teach us how to taste
Delicious blessings you on us bestow:
Fruits of the Spirit, nevermore to waste—
That we from love to love may grow and grow.

EMBRACING OUR CAUSE

A Ritual of Commitment to Justice

This is written for a person or persons who wish to publicly commit to working for justice for lesbian, gay, bisexual, and transgendered people, both in the church and in society. The liturgy may be read responsively, possibly sharing leadership, or antiphonally.

Readings   Exodus 3:1–12; Esther 4:6–16

Reflections

(Reflections may be inward and silent, or spoken [homily or dialogue], sung, dramatized, danced, or omitted.)

Leader: Sometimes God gives us a visible sign such as a burning bush to call us to commitment. But often, the only visible signs that call us are the circumstances of injustice.

People: **We must turn to see the signs of our times. We must turn to listen for God's voice.**

Leader: *N.!* Remove the sandals from your feet, for the place on which you are standing is holy ground.

N.: *Here I am, Sovereign God.* (Removes shoes)

People: **I am the God of your fathers and mothers, the God of Abraham and Sarah and the God of Mary and Joseph, the God of Ruth and Naomi and the God of Jonathan and David. I have observed the misery of my Rainbow people: I have heard their cry, I know their sufferings, I have come to deliver them. So come, I will send you to bring my people, my lesbian, gay, bisexual, and transgendered people, out of oppression.**

N.: *Who am I that I should bring your Rainbow people out of oppression?*

People: **I will be with you; and this shall be the sign for you that it is I who sent you: when you have brought the people out of oppression, you all shall worship here together.**

N.:   *You know what happens to those who go uninvited into the courts of power and stand up for the oppressed!*

People: **Do not think that in this place of worship you will escape injustice. Who knows? Perhaps you have been created for such a time and place as this!**

N.:   *Then fast and pray with me, and I will work for justice. If my well-being is threatened, so be it.*

Hymn   "Walk With Me"
(Words and Music by John Rice; see next page)

Laying On of Hands

(N. kneel[s]; all gathered lay hands on N. for the commission to justice.)

Leader: You will receive power as the Holy Spirit comes upon you, and you will be God's witness(es) here and to the ends of the earth. *(Acts 1:8)*

People: **See, I make you as God to those who oppress. To the oppressed you will bring light and gladness, joy and honor.** *(Exodus 7:1; Esther 8:16)*

The Prayer That Jesus Taught Us

Leader: Let us pray.
People: **God, Father and Mother of us all,**
            hallowed be thy name.
            Thy kingdom come,
            thy will be done,
            on earth as it is in heaven.
            Give us this day our daily bread;
            And forgive us our debts,
            as we forgive our debtors;
            And lead us not into temptation,
            but deliver us from evil.
            For thine is the kingdom, and the power,
            and the glory, forever. Amen.

Walk With Me

Tune: GLASER

John S. Rice

John S. Rice

♩ = 100

Chorus

Walk with me, I will walk with you And build the land that God has planned Where love shines through.

RECLAIMING OUR BAPTISM

Turning the Church Upside Down

This ritual is intended to sacramentalize the redefining of our relationship with the church. It may commemorate separation from current church policies rather than separation from the church, being "in" but not "of" the church, as Jesus called his disciples to be "in" but not "of" the world (John 17:11–14). It may also signify a decision to leave a particular denomination or the institutional church altogether.

To drink one's baptism is to internalize it, honoring our participation in the church universal that is found both within and outside the institutional church. In turning our baptismal waters "upside down" to drink them, we remember how early Christians were accused of turning the world upside down, including the religious structures of their time (Acts 17:6).

(To prepare, fill the baptismal font with water. Place one cup or chalice on the Communion table for every person choosing to renew their baptism in this way.)

(The liturgy may be read responsively, possibly sharing leadership, or antiphonally.)

Opening Words
(Ephesians 4:1–6, 14–16)

Leader: I beg you to lead a life worthy of the calling to which you have been called, with all humility and gentleness, with patience, bearing with one another in love, making every effort to maintain the unity of the Spirit in the bond of peace.

People: **There is one body and one Spirit, just as you were called to the one hope of your calling, one Sovereign,**

one faith, one baptism, one God, Father and Mother of all, who is above all and through all and in all.

Leader: We must no longer be children, tossed to and fro and blown about by every wind of doctrine, by people's trickery, by their craftiness in deceitful scheming.

People: **But speaking the truth in love, we must grow up in every way into the one who is the head, into Christ, promoting the body's growth by building ourselves up in love.**

Leader: Jesus warned his disciples, however: "If anyone will not welcome you or listen to your words, shake off the dust from your feet as you leave that house or town.

People: **"Truly I tell you, it will be more tolerable for the land of Sodom and Gomorrah on the day of judgment than for that town."** (*Matthew 10:14–15*)

Leader: "Yet know this: the commonwealth of God has come near." (*Luke 10:11b*)

Hymn "Once to Every One and Nation"
(*Change "man" to "one"; "His" to "God's."*)

or

"Here I Am, Lord"

Readings Matthew 3:13–17; Acts 10:44–48

Reflections

(*Reflections may be inward and silent, or spoken [homily or dialogue], sung, dramatized, danced, or omitted.*)

Shaking the Dust
and Receiving the Water
(*From Luke 10:34–42*)

Leader: The person(s) redefining (her/his/their) relationship with the [name the specific denomination] church may gather

around this Communion table and offer the responses that
follow. Jesus said, "Do not think that I have come to bring
peace to the earth; I have not come to bring peace, but a
sword."

N.:   *For Christ has set us against our own church, and our*
           foes have been members of our own church family.

Leader: Whoever loves the church more than Christ is not worthy
           of Christ. Whoever does not take up the cross and follow
           Christ is not worthy of Christ.

N.:   *Those who find their life will lose it, and those who lose*
           their life for Christ's sake will find it.

Leader: Whoever welcomes you welcomes Christ, and whoever
           welcomes Christ welcomes the One who sent Christ.

N.:   (I/We) *shake from* (my/our) *feet the dust of those who*
           have not welcomed (me/us/our sisters and brothers).
           (Stomp feet.)

Leader: It will be more tolerable for the land of Sodom and Go-
           morrah on the day of judgment than for those who have
           rejected you or those you love.

People: **Yet know this: the commonwealth of God has come**
           near.

Leader: Truly I tell you, whoever gives you a cup of water to drink
           because you bear the name of Christ will by no means lose
           the reward. (*Mark 9:41*)

(Pre-assigned leaders in the congregation take the cups from the
Communion table and dip them into the baptismal font and return
to the table. One at a time, the leaders give a cup of water to those
redefining their relationship with the church. As each drinks all of
it, the leader should say:)

Leader: You are God's beloved (daughter/son); with you God is
           well pleased.

(After each has received:)

Leader: Those who drink of the water that Christ gives will never
           be thirsty.

People: **The water that Christ gives will become in them a spring of living water gushing up to eternal life.** (*John 4:14*)

Leader: Let us pray.

People: **O God, now let your servants depart in peace, according to your word; for their eyes have seen your salvation which you have prepared in the presence of all peoples, a light for revelation to strangers, and for glory to your people of faith. Amen.** (*Luke 2:29–32*)

Leader: May the peace of Christ be with you!

People: **And also with you!**

(*Offer one another the peace of Christ.*)

Hymn   "Come, Thou Long-Expected Jesus"

(*Tune: Hyfrydol. Text of "Come, Thou Long-Expected Jesus," by Charles Wesley [1744], adaptation. Copyright © 1998 by Chris R. Glaser. Permission granted for use in worship with attribution.*)

Come, thou long-expected Jesus,
Born to set thy people free;
From our fears and bonds release us,
Let us find your liberty.
Our own strength and consolation,
Hope of all the earth thou art;
Dear desire of every station,
Joy of every loving heart.

Born thy people to deliver,
Born to hallow body-soul,
Born to open up our closets
Born to lead, not to control.
Keep us "from weak resignation
To the ills that we deplore":
Guide us in thy common purpose,
To our home, become the door.

CELEBRATING THE COMMONWEALTH

A Rite of God's Victory

This version of Communion may be observed either in antici-
pation of, or as a result of, a victory of God's commonwealth.
Bread and wine (or grape juice) are on the table, which may be
draped with a rainbow flag.

The liturgy may be read responsively, possibly sharing leadership, or antiphonally.

Opening Words
(Revelation 21:1–5)

Leader: Then I saw a new heaven and a new earth; for the first
heaven and the first earth had passed away, and the sea
was no more.
People: **And I saw the holy city, the new Jerusalem, coming
down out of heaven from God.**
Leader: And I heard a loud voice from the throne saying:
People: **See, the home of God is among mortals. God will dwell
with them as their God; they will be God's peoples,
and God will be with them, wiping every tear from
their eyes. Death will be no more; mourning and crying and pain will be no more, for the former things
have passed away.**
Leader: And the one who was seated on the throne said,
People: **"See, I am making all things new."**

Hymn   "God of Our Hearts"

*(New words for the tune Joanna ["Immortal, Invisible, God Only
Wise"] Copyright © 1998 by Chris R. Glaser. Permission granted
for use in worship with attribution.)*

All-loving, embracing, O God of our hearts,
You hurt with us, laugh with us, teach us your arts;

Your sacred creation you give us to tend,
And then your own Body and Spirit you send.

Great giver of mercy and author of love,
Bless those who would follow your long-suffering love:
The Lover you gave us we nailed to a tree,
But Love resurrected in your victory.

Emblazoned in heavens, embodied in earth,
God, bless those who love with repeated rebirth
Past brutal rejections to welcomes of love
And blessings from you—the descent of a dove.

Reading   Ephesians 2:8–22

Reflections

(*Reflections may be inward and silent, or spoken [homily or dialogue], sung, dramatized, danced, or omitted.*)

Invitation to the Table
(*From Ephesians 2:8–22*)

Leader: Friends, we are a dwelling place for God.
People: **We are no longer strangers or sojourners, for by grace we have been saved through faith.**
Leader: For Christ is our peace: in his body and in his blood Christ has united us as one flesh overcoming our dividing walls of hostility.
People: **Through Christ we have access in one Spirit to God. Christ proclaimed peace to those near and to those far so that all of us may know our citizenship in the commonwealth of God, members of the household of God.**
Leader: Christ Jesus is our cornerstone: In Christ we are joined together as a holy temple for our God.

Leader: According to Matthew,
    while the disciples ate,
    Jesus took a loaf of bread,
    and after blessing it, broke it,
    giving it to the disciples with these words:

People: **"Take, eat; this is my body."**

Leader: Then he took the cup, and after giving thanks Jesus gave it to them, saying,

People: **"Drink from it, all of you; for this is my blood of the covenant, which is poured out for many for the forgiveness of sins.**

Leader: I tell you, I will never again drink of this fruit of the vine until that day when I drink it new with you in the commonwealth of God." (*Matthew 26:26–29*)

The Thanksgiving
(*Psalm 126, adapted*)

Leader: When our God restored the fortunes of Zion, we were like those who dream.

People: **Then our mouth was filled with laughter, and our tongue with shouts of joy;**

Leader: Then it was said among the nations, "God has done great things for them."

People: **God has done great things for us, and we rejoice.**

Leader: Those who have sown in tears have reaped a bountiful harvest,

People: **Those who went out weeping have come home with shouts of joy.**

Hymn "For All the Saints"

(*Recommended: Omit the verse that begins "O may thy soldiers . . ."; and also omit "And when the strife is fierce. . . ." Change the concluding phrase of the verse that begins "From earth's wide bounds . . ." to "Praising Creator, Christ, and Holy Ghost."*)

(These verses may be added after the verse that begins, "O blest communion . . .":)

> And as we march around the church's walls
> May we detect their distant trumpet calls
> Cheering our victory as division falls.
> Alleluia! Alleluia!
>
> Thou Holy Spirit, giver of our dream:
> A commonwealth, for our shared esteem,
> And reformation, truth's more light to beam.
> Alleluia! Alleluia!

(Copyright © 1998 by Chris R. Glaser. Permission granted for use in worship with attribution.)

The Prayer That Jesus Taught Us

Leader: Let us pray.
People: **God, Father and Mother of us all,**
      hallowed be thy name.
      Thy kingdom come,
      thy will be done,
      on earth as it is in heaven.
      Give us this day our daily bread;
      And forgive us our debts,
      as we forgive our debtors;
      And lead us not into temptation,
      but deliver us from evil.
      For thine is the kingdom, and the power,
      and the glory, forever. Amen.
Leader: The gifts of God for the people of God!
People: **Thanks be to God!**

Distribution of the Gifts

(After all have received, the service continues:)

Closing Prayer
(*Luke 1:46–55*)

Leader: Our soul magnifies the Sovereign, and our spirits rejoice in God our Savior.

People: **For God has regarded our low estate. Behold, all generations will call us blessed.**

Leader: For God who is mighty has done great things for us, and holy is God's name.

People: **God's mercy is on those in awe of God from generation to generation**

Leader: God has shown strength, scattering the proud in the imagination of their hearts,

People: **Putting down the mighty from their thrones, and exalting those of low degree;**

Leader: Filling the hungry with good things, and sending the rich away empty.

People: **God has delivered us, remembering the mercy prophesied to our mothers and fathers in faith.**

Benediction
(*Numbers 6:24–26, adapted*)

Leader: God has blessed you and kept you;
God has made God's face to shine upon you,
    and been gracious to you;
God has lifted up God's countenance upon you,
    and given you peace.

People: **Go with God's blessing,
Go by God's grace,
Go in God's peace.
Alleluia! Amen!**

Hymn   "Now Thank We All Our God"

(Tune: Nun Danket. "Now Thank We All Our God"; new words Copyright © 1998 by Chris R. Glaser. Permission granted for use in worship with attribution.)

> Now thank we all our God
> For giving our love voices
> And hearts to join its song,
> In this, our God rejoices;
> For this, a covenant—
> A blessing for our world
> And those who march beneath
> A rainbow flag unfurled.
>
> We praise our wondrous God
> For giving us this moment
> Of water turned to wine
> And wine into atonement,
> For body, blood bestowed
> Not only from above,
> But from the flesh of earth
> Comes God's redemptive love.

CONCLUSION

Much of the church claims that the sacrifice of lesbian, gay, bisexual, and transgendered people is necessary to preserve the unity of Christ's Body, the church. The reality is that Christ's Body is already broken by homophobia and heterosexism. Our living sacrament of coming out, whose multiple dimensions are ritualized in this chapter, serves to unmask yet further the sacrificial violence inherent in "us" and "them" mimetic rivalry and scapegoating. Our vulnerability makes at-one-ment possible among straight, gay, lesbian, bisexual, and transgendered Christians. We follow Jesus, called out to reveal our sacred worth and to offer our lives as gifts to others by a God who desires mercy, not sacrifice.

Selected Bibliography

Alexander, Marilyn Bennett, and James Preston. *We Were Baptized Too: Claiming God's Grace for Lesbians and Gays.* Louisville, Ky.: Westminster John Knox Press, 1996.

Boswell, John. *Christianity, Social Tolerance, and Homosexuality: Gay People in Western Europe from the Beginning of the Christian Era to the Fourteenth Century.* Chicago: University of Chicago Press, 1980.

Campbell, Joseph, with Bill Moyers. *The Power of Myth.* New York: Doubleday & Co., 1988.

Chauncey, George. *Gay New York: Gender, Urban Culture, and the Making of the Gay Male World, 1890–1940.* New York: Basic Books, 1994.

Dix, Dom Gregory. *The Shape of the Liturgy.* London: Dacre Press, 1945.

Girard, René. *Violence and the Sacred.* Translated by Patrick Gregory. Baltimore: Johns Hopkins University Press, 1977.

———. *The Scapegoat.* Translated by Yvonne Freccero. Baltimore: Johns Hopkins University Press, 1986.

Heyward, Carter. *Touching Our Strength: The Erotic as Power and the Love of God.* San Francisco: Harper & Row, 1989.

Nouwen, Henri J. M. *The Inner Voice of Love: A Journey through Anguish to Freedom.* New York: Doubleday & Co., 1996.

O'Neill, Craig, and Kathleen Ritter. *Coming Out Within: Stages of Spiritual Awakening for Lesbians and Gay Men.* San Francisco: HarperSanFrancisco, 1992.

Sloyan, Gerard S. *The Crucifixion of Jesus: History, Myth, Faith.* Minneapolis: Fortress Press, 1995.

Williams, James G. *The Bible, Violence, and the Sacred: Liberation from the Myth of Sanctioned Violence.* Valley Forge, Pa: Trinity Press International, 1991.

Winter, Michael. *The Atonement.* Problems in Theology Series. Collegeville, Minn.: Liturgical Press, 1995.